To Emanuela

Be Grounded in Jesus Name

Grounded

Building a Firm Foundation in Christ

Emmanuel Adeseko

Grounded: Building a Firm Foundation in Christ

Cover design by Stephen Davis

Copyright © 2016 Emmanuel Adeseko

ISBN-13: 978-1537781181

ISBN-10: 1537781189

Printed in the United Kingdom

Published by CreateSpace

CONTENTS

ACKNOWLEDGEMENTS

My deepest appreciation goes to the following people:

My mother, Bridget — Your prayers and encouragement have helped to make me the person I am today. Thank you for all your support and for sharing your dreams, which have encouraged me to keep going. I love you!

My brothers, George and James — Both of you are beyond precious to me. Thank you for your support and being the amazing brothers you guys are. You are part of my inspiration for writing. You are both amazing!

Uncle Victor and Aunty Helen — There are no words to express how grateful I am to have you in my life. Your support and prayers for my family and the guidance you have given is beyond words. Thank you and God bless you!

Apostle Michael Stephens — You have witnessed my weaknesses and walked with me during some difficult times in my life. I appreciate you and pray God blesses you greatly sir. Thank you!

Pastor Timothy Adelegan — You have been a great encouragement in my life. Both in strength and weakness you have been like a brother and most of all, a blessing. Thank you!

Teresa Manu — Your encouragement and support goes beyond words. You truly have become like a sister to me. I love and appreciate you dearly! Thank you!

Charlene France — Thank you for all your support and encouragement. Your help with hours of editing and proof-reading have been a blessing! Thank you!

New Covenant Ministries Team — Thank you all for your support, encouragement and helpful attitude. I love each of you very much!

Most importantly, my sincere gratitude to my Father God. It's because of you that all of this has been possible. Even when I feel unworthy, your love and grace empower me to do what you have called me to do. You have done too much for me Father. Thank you. I am forever grateful and will love you forever!

INTRODUCTION

'As you therefore have received Christ Jesus the Lord, so walk in Him, rooted and built up in Him and established in the faith, as you have been taught, abounding in it with thanksgiving.' — Colossians 2:6-7

One of the most important aspects of a building is its foundation. Builders can spend significant time digging far below ground level to lay a foundation that is both secure and able to stand in the midst of all weather conditions.

Over the past ten years of serving God in various forms of ministry, it has been amazing to see lives transformed by the Gospel. One key experience was when I served within a pastoral team while there was an outpouring of the Holy Spirit that brought many young people to Christ. Many of them were radically transformed by the power of the Gospel. Unfortunately however, some turned away from following Jesus. The latter baffled me and I asked God a simple question: 'Jesus, how can people completely deny You after experiencing Your presence and power so obviously?' It was this question that I feel provoked the next stage of events. In February 2010, I then had a vision of people being examined before the throne of God. They appeared as buildings that varied in quality and design. Some buildings had a roof but no door structure. Others were beautiful but made of poor materials. Others were robust and paved with gold and precious metal. It was as if Jesus was examining them before they entered into the glory of God. After having this experience, it further fuelled a desire to understand what the foundations of Christian Faith are and why they are significant. The Holy Spirit placed the following scripture on my heart after this vision:

Therefore leaving the discussion of the elementary principles of Christ, let us go on towards perfection, not laying again the foundation of repentance from dead works and of faith towards God, of doctrine of baptisms, of laying on of hands, of resurrection of the dead and of eternal judgments. And this we will do if God permits' — Hebrews 6:1-3

Introduction

Elements are essential characteristics of something abstract or tangible. In Hebrews 6:1-2 several topics are mentioned; repentance, faith towards God, baptisms, laying on of hands, the resurrection of the dead and the eternal judgement. These can collectively be understood as 'the elementary principles of Christ.' As I began to explore and apply the principles to these topics, there was a significant impact on my relationship with Jesus and impact on the Gospel. I was also reminded of this amazing scripture below:

> 'The Lord has appeared of old to me, saying: "Yes, I have loved you with an everlasting love; Therefore with loving-kindness I have drawn you. Again I will build you, and you shall be rebuilt, O virgin of Israel! You shall again be adorned with your tambourines, and shall go forth in the dances of those who rejoice.' — Jeremiah 31:3-4

The historical context of the verse above is that Israel had experienced sorrow and desolation due to their disobedience to God. However God promised restoration to His people, declaring that His love is not limited to time but indeed is 'everlasting'. He assures them that regardless of their present condition He will draw His people back to Himself by His Spirit. He declares that He will build them and rebuild them. This has great application for us today.

God's love for you is everlasting. Regardless of whether you are a new Christian, have been walking with the Lord for a long time or have lost your faith, God will build you and rebuild you. He builds new foundations and restores broken ones. That is the objective of this book: building a secure foundation in Christ Jesus.

An overview of each topic will be covered chapter by chapter and I would encourage you to read each section in order. Search the scriptures on each page and explore the study guide prayerfully to gain further understanding and revelation from the Holy Spirit. I pray that as you read this book you will be energized and filled with the spirit of wisdom and revelation that you may be grounded in the knowledge of your inheritance through Christ Jesus. May you be built up in Him that you may go onto perfection in Jesus Name. Amen.

CHAPTER 1: SALVATION

'Nor is there salvation in any other, for there is no other name under heaven given among men by which we must be saved.' — Acts 4:12

INTRODUCTION

There is no greater love, courage or value a person can place on us than to go out of their way to rescue us. We celebrate firefighters for their acts of courage when saving men and women from burning buildings. We acknowledge brave men and women that risk their lives to fight for their country. However, the Gospel is the greatest story of rescue from danger in the history of creation. What is salvation? Why do we need to be saved? How can we be saved? Is it worth it? In this chapter, we will answer these questions as we explore the free, yet priceless gift God has given us.

WHAT IS SALVATION?

The Greek word for salvation is 'sozo', which means to heal, to preserve, deliver, to rescue or to make safe. Salvation describes the act of saving someone from harm and then putting him or her into safety. The whole point of being rescued is that you recognise your inability to free yourself from harm. This means relying on the power of another to deliver you from danger and into a place of safety. See the passage below:

'What man of you, having a hundred sheep, if he loses one of them, does not leave the ninety-nine in the wilderness, and go after the one which is lost until he finds it? And when he has found it, he lays it on his shoulders, rejoicing. And when he comes home, he calls together his friends and neighbors, saying to them, 'Rejoice with me, for I have found my sheep which was lost!' — Luke 15:4-6

Salvation is both an event and process of rescue. Jesus used this parable to highlight some simple yet profound truths. Did you notice that the shepherd is seeking the sheep? This is symbolic of God's pursuit of humanity, seeking and searching. In Christianity, we are primarily the pursued and not the pursuer. This breaks religious thinking immediately because in traditional religion man is searching for God, rather than being search for by God. We are invited to simply respond to what God has done. Jesus portrays humanity as the 'lost sheep'. We are the ones that have no power, knowledge or good deeds to save ourselves. All we can do is cooperate with the Shepherd in his rescue. This is the Gospel: God rescuing humankind from the penalty and power of sin (danger) and bringing believers into His provision and Kingdom (safety). For us to grasp how great this salvation is, we must first look at how God intended things to be in the beginning.

WHAT WAS GOD'S PLAN FOR MAN?

'When I consider Your heavens, the work of Your fingers, The moon and the stars, which You have ordained, What is man that You are mindful of him, And the son of man that You visit him? For you have made Him a little lower than the angels (God), and you have crowned him with glory and honour. You have made him to have dominion over the works of Your hands; You have put all things under his feet, All sheep and oxen—Even the beasts of the field, the birds of the air, and the fish of the sea that pass through the paths of the seas.' —
Psalm 8:3-8

God did not create us for religion but for relationship. We were never created to be slaves of God. Neither were we created to have a long distance relationship with Him based on solemn ceremonies. In fact, God does not believe in long distance relationships. We can learn several things from the first account of God's creation and interaction with man in Genesis (see Genesis 1-3).

'God did not create us for religion but for relationship.'

God created man for communion

Man was created to live in fellowship with God. God did not create man for religion but relationship. The definition of communion is 'the sharing or exchanging of intimate thoughts and feelings, especially on a mental or spiritual level'. The first relationship man ever had was with God, his Father. Even in the midst of all the animals and creatures, Adam lived before the audience of One. From this, we see a picture of what worship looked like; Adam became what he beheld. As He looked into the face of His Father, Adam reflected God's glory. Adam's education came from his divine encounter and fellowship with God. In Psalm 8, it says that God is 'mindful' of man and 'visited' him. Mindful describes God's countless thoughts and consideration for man (Psalm 139:17-18). Man was not a mere slave but a son. When Psalm 8 says that God 'visited man,' it is relating to the interaction between God and man in The Garden of Eden. There was no evidence of lifeless religious activity but instead a record of an intimate relationship between God and man. God would meet man and have communion with him. Consideration, visitation and habitation – this was the summary of activity between God and man. Adam was the temple God dwelt in. He was Gods habitation.

God made man for dominion

The earth was the territory that man was created to rule on behalf of God. Man was created to represent God on earth and rule over all of God's creation (Genesis 1:26). In Psalm 8 it says that God *'made him to have dominion over the works of your hands; you have put all things under his feet, All sheep and oxen—Even the beasts of the field'*. The word dominion in Hebrew is *'radah'* which means to tread down, subdue, rule or prevail. Because man was in relationship with God, he could represent God's authority on earth. Dominion was the highest expression of Adams worship. Just as God created the world with His word, He also transferred this creative power to Adam to name in The Garden of Eden (Genesis 2:19). All of creation was subject to man's authority because he was created in God's image (Genesis 1:26). Fathers provide the image for their children (Genesis 1:26, 5:2). Just as Adam inherited Gods image, so also would his children inherit his image.

God made Earth to be a reflection of Heaven

In Genesis 2:7, it says that 'God breathed into man the breath of life.' This teaches us that not only was Adam born from above but also his life began when the Spirit of God entered him. All of God's attributes were in His Spirit, which was 'breathed' into man. This enabled him to think and act in harmony with God. This tells us that real life begins when we are filled with His Spirit. Through the Spirit of God, he could reflect heaven on earth. God always intended for the earth to be governed by a spirit filled man with heavenly thinking.

Man was to be crowned with Glory and Honour

How did he rule over the things of God? The scripture above tells us that he was 'crowned with glory and honour.' The Hebrew word for glory is 'Kahbod', which means splendour, wealth, honour and weight. One principle we learn from Adam's fellowship with God in Eden is this: you become whatever you behold. As Adam beheld God's glory, he could reflect it perfectly. Adam could reflect God's nature because God was the focus of Adam's worship. Not only was man crowned with glory but he was also filled with glory (Genesis 2:7). It was the glory that enabled man to represent God on the earth. It is important to note that only the righteous can carry glory. Because man was righteous, he could live in fellowship with God and carry His glory.

WHAT WAS THE IMPACT OF SIN?

'Whoever commits sin also commits lawlessness, and sin is lawlessness.' — 1 John 3:4

Sin is lawlessness. There are two aspects — Sin (the root) and sins (the fruit). Sin is the lawless nature that is against God's holy and righteous nature, which we inherited from Adam. Sins are the actions that are produced because of having a sinful state. It creates an evil nature that violates the Holy and righteous character of God. By disobedience, they fell from their sinless state through the temptation by Satan. In Genesis 3 we see this temptation is founded and operates upon deception. The story of Adam and Eve in the Garden of Eden teaches us that Satan's plan is to deceive men into thinking that they can be like God without actually submitting to Him. Here are three ways that sin impacted man:

Breaks communion with God

'They heard the sound of the Lord God walking in the garden in the cool of the day, and Adam and his wife hid themselves from the presence of the Lord God'. Genesis 3:8

'God is love and so sin makes man run from Love'

As soon as sin entered, fellowship with God stopped. God then asked Adam 'where are you?' God asked the question not because He did not know the answer, but because He wanted man to realise what sin does to our fellowship with God. Sin takes you to places you do not want to go. Out of light and into darkness. Sin breaks fellowship with God and costs Adam to lose intimacy with Him. Sin teaches fear, and fear makes man run from God. God is love and so sin makes man run from Love. We see the impact of this in society today. People have a misconception of what love looks like because they have not taken insight from the true source of love — God.

Distorted man's perception of God and himself

Another word used to describe sin is iniquity. In Hebrew, it is 'avon', which means to pervert, make crooked and to twist. This is exactly what sin did to the image of God inside of man's heart and mind. It corrupted the image that man was formed in, and twisted our perception of who God is. In fact, Colossians 1:21 says that man became an '...enemy of God in his mind through wicked works.' Creation only submitted to Adam's authority because he was made in the image of God. As soon as God's image within Adam was corrupted by sin, he lost the power to rule. Creation no longer recognised his authority because God's image within Adam was corrupted. Adam was also a father. He then transferred this sinful image to all generations after him. His children inherited the same evil nature and therefore all offspring were born into sin (Genesis 5:1-3, Romans 3:23).

Sin brings corruption, sickness, uncleanness and death

In Romans 6:23 it says 'For the wages of sin is death.' The consequences of sin are deadly. Through sin, death spreads to all men. Uncleanness, corruption and all kinds of diseases came into the world through sin (Romans 5:11-12). There are two kinds of death: physical and spiritual. Physical death is when the body dies. Spiritual death is when the spirit becomes separated from God in a state of isolation and torment. Spiritual death is the eternal absence of God's presence and communion with Him. Of these two kinds of death, the spiritual version is far worse! The cost of sin is more than anyone would be willing to pay; it costs your communion with God, your inheritance and your eternity! Death is the tragic payment for sin (Romans 6:23).

WHAT WAS GODS RESPONSE?

> *'Atonement; removing man's sin in order for him to be restored back into fellowship with God.'*

Although He loves man, God hates sin and cannot have fellowship with him if he remains in his sinful state. God's purity would destroy sin, which means that if a man with a sinful nature comes into God's presence he will die. God's holy and righteous nature demands justice against sin (Psalm 97:2, Romans 1:32). To restore man back to life in communion with God, God needed to deal with and cover his sin. This is called atonement; removing man's sin for him to be restored back into fellowship with God.

God gave various pictures in the Old Testament to portray His plan to rescue man from the consequences of sin, and make atonement for him forever. One example of this is in the tabernacle of Moses (Exodus 25-40), for which the blood of lambs and bulls provided a temporary covering (atonement) for man's sin (Leviticus 1-3). The animal was a substitute for the worshiper. The worshiper would confess his sins while laying hands on the lamb. The lamb would be killed on an altar before God and its blood would be shed as a sacrifice for their sin. If done properly the sins of the worshiper would be transferred onto the victim. The innocence of the victim would be transferred on to the worshiper. It was symbolic of the horror of sin and gave the people the understanding that someone would have to die for the people to stand in the presence of God without guilt of sin. Worship was more than a song, it symbolised a life given for a life. God was painting a picture that pointed to His final plan to bring salvation and make an eternal covering (atonement) for the sins of humanity.

WHY WAS JESUS BORN?

Sin was the problem. Jesus is the answer. Nevertheless, why is He the answer? Let us look at why Jesus was born and how he fulfilled God's plan of salvation for humanity.

Deliver man from sin

> *'And she will bring forth a Son, and you shall call His name Jesus, for He will save His people from their sins.' Matthew 1:21*

In the Hebrew culture names were given as a prayer towards God and as a memorial of the experiences of the people (Genesis 4:25,6:29, 1 Samuel 4:21). Names were also given to reveal the identity, purpose and destiny of the character of the individual that was born. The name Jesus in Hebrew is 'Yeshua', which means 'God is my salvation' and is a key reason why the Father sent His Son into the world (John 3:16). God delivered us from the penalty of sin through the sacrifice of Jesus Christ on The Cross. The salvation we have through faith in Jesus is threefold: justification, sanctification and glorification. Justification means that we have been delivered from the penalty of sin (Romans 5:9). Sanctification means that we are being delivered from the power of sins' influence on our souls (John 17:17, James 1:21). Glorification means that we will be delivered from the presence of sin entirely (Romans 8:18, Revelations 7:16). He is the Lamb that God provided to make eternal covering (atonement) for our sins once and for all! The Cross served as the altar and Jesus became the sacrifice. Hebrews explains the limitations of the Aaronic priests to make offerings atone for the people, but Jesus' blood has the power to cleanse us from all sin and He forever lives to make intercession for us, praise God! The new covenant between God and man is made through the blood of Jesus Christ. He is also the mediator of the new covenant (Hebrews 9:15).

Reveal the Father

> 'Philip said to Him, 'Lord, show us the Father, and it is
> sufficient for us. 'Jesus said to him, 'Have I been with you so
> long, and yet you have not known Me, Philip? He who has
> seen me has seen the Father; so how can you say, 'Show us
> the Father'? Do you not believe that I am in the Father, and
> the Father in Me? The words that I speak to you I do not
> speak on my own authority; but the Father who dwells in me
> does the works.' — John 14:8-10

Jesus had been with His disciples for about three years, the disciples then asked Him 'show us the Father.' They did not realize that His whole life drew a picture of who the Father is and what He is like. The fullness of God is in Jesus; He spent over 30 years demonstrating the Father's heart towards His creation. Though they had been God's chosen people, their perception of the Father became perverted by their sinful nature and therefore they could only worship Him from a distance. Not only was Jesus the Son sent to save us from sin, but also to reveal the face of the Father.

To reconcile man with God

> 'For if when we were enemies we were reconciled to God
> through the death of His Son, much more, having been
> reconciled, we shall be saved by His life.' — Romans 5:10

'We are united with the Father through faith in his Son by the power of the Holy Spirit.'

God not only sent His Son Jesus to reveal the Father but to reconcile us to Him. The word 'reconcile' means 'put people back on friendly terms, end conflict, to make some-body accept something or to make something compatible'. This is what Jesus did for us on The Cross! Jesus ended the conflict between man and God; He restored communion and dominion to humankind, praise God! A divine exchange took place on The Cross; our sins transferred to Jesus and His righteousness gifted to us by grace through faith. Colossians 2:14 says, 'having wiped out the handwriting of requirements that was against us, which was contrary to us. And He has taken it out of the way, having nailed it to the cross'. Our sin was condemned on The Cross. In fact, God judged His Son on The Cross so that we could be made righteous sons through faith in Jesus! Hallelujah! We are united with the Father through faith in His Son by the power of the Holy Spirit!

Restore man to Glory

'And the glory which You gave Me I have given them, that they may be one just as We are one' — John 17:22

A minister once said 'what Adam lost; we have gained through Jesus with interest.' This is more than true! In John 17, Jesus' prayer highlights that we have been given His glory. However, the glory that Jesus restored is greater than the glory Adam lost. Not only did He obtain this glory but He also clothed us in it. Through Christ we 'crowned with glory and honour' again (Hebrews 2:5-9).

WHO ARE YOU NOW?

You are a saint! A saint is 'sanctus' in Latin, which means someone who is made holy. You have been forgiven of all your sins! The blood of Jesus has delivered you from the penalty of sin and power

'You are God's son through faith in Christ Jesus.'

of death. It no longer has dominion over you (Romans 6:13). Your history has been erased and you have inherited Christ's identity, nature and kingdom. You have been crucified with Christ and are now alive unto God through faith in Him (Galatians 2:20). You are Gods temple and the Holy Spirit dwells within you (1 Corinthians 6:19-20). You are a supernatural being with supernatural abilities. You have been restored to live in fellowship with God, which leads to eternal life! (John 17:3). You have an eternal purpose and have been brought into the ministry of reconciliation. This means you can connect others to God the Father by sharing the Gospel of Jesus (2 Corinthians 5:21). Not only do we have access into God's presence but also His presence has full access unto us. You are God's son through faith in Christ Jesus. You are called, to no longer live merely for yourself but for God, the Father of our Lord Jesus Christ. He is the Saviour of our souls. Through Jesus, we have been redeemed out of the hand of the devil and have been delivered into the Kingdom of God (Colossians 1:13). The Cross was not a tragedy, it is Heavens greatest victory.

HOW DO YOU RESPOND TO THE GOSPEL?

'That if you confess with your mouth the Lord Jesus and believe in your heart that God has raised Him from the dead, you will be saved. For with the heart one believes unto righteousness, and with the mouth confession is made unto salvation. For the Scripture says, 'Whoever believes in Him will not be put to shame.' For there is no distinction between Jew and Greek, for the same Lord over all is rich to all who call upon Him. For 'whoever calls on the name of the Lord shall be saved.' — Romans 10:8-10.

'The time is fulfilled, and the kingdom of God is at hand. Repent, and believe in the gospel.' — mark 1:15

Turn from sin and trust in Jesus. Those who have received Jesus to be their Lord and Saviour will produce a life of obedience to God and love for His people (1 John 2:6). As we walk with Him, we will no longer bear the fruit of sin but of righteousness. It is vital for you to understand that salvation is not the End but the Beginning. God's objective is to make you and I like Christ. Christ is the Way, Truth and Life. He is the car, the route and the destination all at the same time. Salvation is a means to recreate man inside of Jesus Christ. As you grow in communion with God through prayer, by reading and obeying His word, Christ's nature will be reflected through you. No matter how bright the Moon shines at night, it does not produce its light. It simple reflects light because it is positioned before the sun. All the moon has is a position and because of its position, it can reflect sunlight. This is analogy can be directly applied to our relationship with God through Jesus. That being said, you do not work FOR righteousness, you work FROM it. Christ's death restored the position of righteousness we lost with the Father. Salvation in Christ has transferred us from death to life. We are now rightly placed with God the Father through His Son Jesus. We can now reflect God's glory as we behold Him in prayer and His word (2 Corinthians 3:16-18).

CONCLUSION — BE RECONCILED TO GOD

God does not want a long distance relationship with you. Anything that is worth something will cost something. Jesus paid the price for you on The Cross because God says you are worth it! Your history does not determine your destiny. Jesus' blood wiped your 'DBS' clean through faith in Him. Jesus freed you from your past to inherit His destiny. You are a son and not an orphan. In 2 Corinthians 5:30 it says 'Now then, we are ambassadors for Christ, as though God were pleading through us: we implore you on Christ's behalf, be reconciled to God.' Should you get clean before you bath? Get better before you go to the hospital? Or maybe fix your car before taking it to the garage? No. So how can we think we can 'get right' before coming to God? The Gospel is not DIY (Do it yourself). No matter how long it has been, or how far away, come to Jesus and He will forgive, wash and restore you. God loves you and sent Jesus to pay the price for you. Just as the lost sheep relies on the shepherd for rescue, trust in Jesus and rely on His power to save and keep you.

CHAPTER 1 — SALVATION: PERSONAL STUDY

1. **What does salvation mean? Write a definition in your own words.**

   To be resored onto God

   To be ~~houtfe~~ healed by God

   Hope

2. **Read Luke 15:1-7. What are the key points in the parable of the shepherd? How does this relate to God's plan of salvation for humankind?**

   God's Love for mankind, rejoys over the

   salvation + restoration of each of individual

   Jesus showed that He cares about

   everyone in the world

3. **According to the following verses, what did God create man for? Can you identify any other characteristics?**

   Genesis 1:26-31

   To dominate the earth

   Produce & feed the earth

   Psalm 8:1-9

   Dominion & worship

   Colossians 1:16

   For God /to worship God &

   be used by God

4. According to Leviticus 17:11, what does atonement mean?

Stand in the gap? Sacrifice for?

5. According to the following scriptures, what does sin do?

Isaiah 59:1-2

Stops God from hearing + Seperate us from God

Hebrews 3:11-12

Seperation from God / sin = no salvation

6. Why was Jesus born? List 4 reasons

- To show How to leave live a Holy life
- To sacrifice His blood for me
- Restore relationship between God & man
- God loves us & wants us to return / & accompush His original plan

CHAPTER 2: REPENTANCE

'From that time Jesus began to preach and to say, 'Repent, for the kingdom of heaven is at hand.' — Matthew 4:17

INTRODUCTION

Repentance is not a message of condemnation but restoration. Often it is viewed as a negative or legalistic word but it is at the very beginning of the Gospel. This was the message Jesus began to preach after coming out of the wilderness, which caused many broken sinners to turn to God and trust in Him for salvation. The judgement of God stopped when His people fulfilled repentance in the Old Testament. The churches in the book of Revelation were not advised to be better people or to try harder; they were only told to repent. What then is repentance? Why is it necessary? What does repentance involve and are saints required to do this after placing their faith in Jesus? This chapter will answer these questions as we focus on God's gift of repentance: the key through which we access the fullness of God's kingdom.

WHAT DOES REPENTANCE MEAN?

'Godly repentance involves two things: turning from and turning to.'

The Greek word for repent is 'Metonaia' which means to show regret or guilt. The Hebrew word repent is 'Teshuva' meaning to return. Repentance means to turn; it is the activity of reviewing and changing one's actions/thinking after a feeling of regret/guilt for past wrongs. Godly repentance involves two things; turning from and turning to. Turning from sin, death and Satan and turning to life and salvation, which is found in being reconciled to Father God through Jesus. Tragically, many Christians only understand repentance as turning from sin. This is true but not complete. Repentance is not only about turning from sin, but also restoring Jesus to be the highest treasure and pleasure in our hearts and lives. Have a look at the following scripture:

> *'But what do you think? A man had two sons, and he came to the first and said, 'Son, go, work today in my vineyard.' He answered and said, 'I will not,' but afterward he regretted it and went. Then he came to the second and said likewise. And he answered and said, 'I go, sir,' but he did not go. Which of the two did the will of his father?' They said to Him, 'The first.' 'Jesus said to them, 'Assuredly, I say to you that tax collectors and harlots enter the kingdom of God before you. For John came to you in the way of righteousness, and you did not believe him; but tax collectors and harlots believed him; and when you saw it, you did not afterward relent and believe him.'' — Matthew 21:28-32*

Jesus used the parable of the father and two sons to explain the concept of repentance. The two sons were asked by their father to work in his vineyard. The first son refused, but later 'regretted it and went'. The second son said that he would go but afterward did not.

The second son had an outward expression of obedience but because of his unchanged heart or mind, he could not carry out the desire of his father. He just gave words or lip service. The first son did not have any outward expression of obedience; in fact, it was clear that he was disobedient. However, his heart and mind were truly changed. This resulted in a change in his actions and obedience to his father. His change came from the inside out. God is not interested in us just doing outward expressions of religious behavior like the Pharisees. These dead works do not produce life. He wants our hearts to be changed through His Word & Holy Spirit. Look at the scripture below:

> *'Therefore the Lord said: 'Inasmuch as these people draw near with their mouths And honour Me with their lips, But have removed their hearts far from Me, And their fear toward Me is taught by the commandment of men'' — Isaiah 29:13*

Jesus quoted this verse when speaking to the Pharisees in Mark 7:6. God does not want us just to change our behavior. The Gospel is not merely about behavior modification. Repentance is a change of heart/thinking that causes us to return to the purpose and plans of God. It is about the turning from death to life. Jesus explained that through repentance anyone could inherit the kingdom of God, even those most unlikely or undeserving. Repentance is a change of heart that causes a reversal of the decision and leads to a change of direction/actions.

WHY DO WE NEED TO REPENT?

'Every way of a man is right in his own eyes, But the Lord weighs the hearts.' — Proverbs 21:2

'For they being ignorant of God's righteousness, and seeking to establish their own righteousness, have not submitted to the righteousness of God. For Christ is the end of the law for righteousness to everyone who believes.' — Romans 10:3-4

Morality is built into the spiritual DNA of humankind. He can even say 'I'm a good person' when comparing himself to other people. This is because of his inherent need to justify his decisions/actions, based on his source of truth and reference for what is right and wrong. Before he fell from glory, his source of righteousness was God Himself. This meant that because God was man's source of life, truth and righteousness God determined what right and wrong was. After man sinned and became separate from God, he became his own source of righteousness (self-righteous). 'Truth' was no longer absolute (from God) but subjective (from man). 'Every way of man is right in his own eyes' because his source of life, truth and righteousness had changed and his conscience was corrupted by sin.

In God's plan of salvation, He was required to rescue man from his self-righteousness, which was leading him to his own destruction (Proverbs 16:25). This involved His pursuit of man to change his heart and recognize his unrighteousness. God brought the Law to reveal a picture of true righteousness but man had no power to fulfil this standard.

The Gospel of Jesus Christ reveals the righteousness and truth of God (Romans 1:17). Jesus began to preach 'repent, for the Kingdom of Heaven is at hand' (Matthew 4:17). Why? Because Jesus was sent to re-establish God's righteousness in the Earth. His righteousness would be gifted to anyone who would turn from sin, self-righteousness and trust in Him for salvation. Man would only receive Jesus' righteousness when he came to a revelation that he is unrighteous before God. When man recognizes this, he then becomes a candidate for the saving grace found through faith in Jesus. We then qualify to access all the fullness of the Kingdom of God. God graciously gives us all that we need through faith in Jesus Christ. This is the blessing and power of the Gospel which is truly good news to all who believe!

ARE THERE BENEFITS OF REPENTANCE?

Because God is love, anything He commands us to do is motivated by love. For you to respond to God's gift of repentance, it is important to understand that repentance itself is a means to an end. It is the doorway that leads to many of God's promises. Repentance has many benefits, some of which are listed below:

Entry into God's Kingdom and access to God's provision

> 'From that time Jesus began to preach and to say, 'Repent, for the kingdom of heaven is at hand.' — Matthew 4:17

Entry into the Kingdom of God is reserved for those who repent. Jesus preached repentance and sinners flocked to Him. Why? Because repentance gave them access into His Kingdom. The Kingdom of God is 'righteousness, peace and joy in the Holy Spirit'. It symbolizes God's reign in the hearts and lives of His people. It represents the dominion that Adam lost and inheritance promised to God's people. Jesus Himself represents the fullness of the Kingdom of God; the King cannot be divided from His kingdom. Jesus brought grace for salvation (John 1:17). This means that repentance makes you a candidate for God's saving grace. This grace brings us into citizenship in God's kingdom and restores us into relationship with the King.

Christian author Roy Hession suggested in his book The Power of God's Grace that 'we enter into the good when we repent of the bad'. This statement is very true and a key principle. If we want to access the things God has for us, we must be humble and acknowledge what we do not have. For

> *'Repentance cannot be a message of condemnation but one of restoration.'*

example, God has promised us peace but to access this, we must express to God 'Father I have no peace.' God will then make us a candidate because we have acknowledged what we do not have. He then graciously gives to us based upon the merits of Jesus' sacrifice of The Cross. Repentance cannot be a message of condemnation but one of restoration.

Restores the presence of God

Repent therefore and be converted, that your sins may be blotted out, so that times of refreshing may come from the presence of the Lord,' — Acts 3:19

Repentance restores the presence of God back into our lives. This enables us to think in line with God, feel in line with God and desire in line with Him. God's presence brings joy (Psalm 16:11). A Christian without God's presence will be truly miserable. The presence of God produces strength. In the Old Testament the ark of God was symbolic of His presence. When the ark was with Israel, the people were empowered to win battles, when the ark was taken they lost (2 Samuel 6). This has much relevance today. If you do not have God's presence, you will be weak and unable to win spiritual battles against the flesh, the world and Satan.

There are at least four dimensions of God's presence mentioned in the Bible:

1   Omnipresence — this is God being everywhere and seeing everything (Proverbs 15:3, Hebrews 4:13).

2   Indwelling presence — this is promised to those who repent and trust in Jesus, which enables Jesus to dwell within us by His Holy Spirit (John 14:15-17).

3   Manifested presence — When God's presence can be felt tangibly in our physical senses (Acts 2:2-4).

4   Dwelling presence — When God's presence remains with a people and place, and changes the spiritual/physical culture to reflect Heaven (Exodus 25:8). The word dwell in Hebrews is 'shakan' which means to dwell or settle. This is where we can get the word 'shekinah' , which means the dwelling glory of God.

God said to Moses in Exodus 33:14 'my presence shall go with you, and I will give you rest.' The presence of God in our lives is a sign of God's approval, comfort, guidance and protection. His presence is a compass and produces His attributes within us (Galatians 5:21-22). Sin will cause the presence of God to depart from a person's life. When a person repents from sin God's presence is restored, which refreshes the soul. Another word that can be used interchangeably with refreshing is revival. Repentance revives the soul.

Access to God's Grace and Mercy

> *Go and proclaim these words toward the north, and say:*
> *'Return, backsliding Israel,' says the Lord; 'I will not cause My*
> *anger to fall on you. For I am merciful,' says the Lord; 'I will*
> *not remain angry forever.' — Jeremiah 3:13*

Repentance invites God's mercy. Mercy is when God withholds from us what we deserve. It is that mercy that inspires us to give our lives to Him (Romans 12:1). After God introduces us to His mercy, we then become recipients of His grace. Grace is when God gives us what should be withheld from us.

ARE THERE DANGERS OF BEING UNREPENTANT?

Yes, the sad truth is that there are terrible consequences for being unrepentant. Consequences can be either immediate or gradual, but they will come. Listed below are some examples:

Reprobate mind

> *'And even as they did not like to retain God in their*
> *knowledge, God gave them over to a debased mind, to do*
> *those things which are not fitting' — Romans 1:28*

Reprobate means 'good for nothing.' A reprobate or debased mind describes a heart so hardened by sin that the conscious is void of moral reasoning or conviction. God pleads with us in Hebrews 3:14 'Today if you will hear his voice, harden not your hearts.' Refusing to respond to your conscious will cause your heart to become hardened. This will eventually result in losing the ability to answer to the conviction of the Holy Spirit. The sad truth of this means you can no longer discern between good and evil. Hebrews 6:6 says: 'they crucify to themselves the Son of God afresh, and put him to an open shame.' Tragically, those who continue to deny His conviction privately will eventually deny communion with Him publically.

Deception

> 'If we say that we have no sin, we deceive ourselves, and the
> truth is not in us.' — 1 John 1:8

Being unrepentant will cause you to view truth from a perspective that has been corrupted by error. Because the person is still in agreement with a lie, their moral compass is corrupted. This is usually how heresy and unbiblical belief systems concerning God are formed. Not only will being unrepentant cause deception, but it will also maintain the deception. If they refuse to repent of any known sin, they prevent God's truth from having access to guide their conscience and they will eventually view truth as a lie.

Judgment or Loss of eternal inheritance

> 'And I gave her time to repent of her sexual immorality, and
> she did not repent. Indeed I will cast her into a sickbed, and
> those who commit adultery with her into great tribulation,
> unless they repent of their deeds.' — Revelation 2:21-22

The reality is not repenting will invite the judgment of God. This can come in different forms. However, unrepentant sin will always lead to the absence of God's presence and the loss of your eternal inheritance. God does not judge us to condemn but to produce repentance.

WHAT ARE THE STAGES OF REPENTANCE?

'Therefore bear fruits worthy of repentance, — Matthew 3:8

John uses a tree as a metaphor to describe the nature of repentance. Repentance is for saints as well as sinners. Just as the fruit of a tree is visible and reveals what kind of tree it is, so also are the signs of repentance. Below are three stages of godly repentance.

Conviction

'And when He has come, He will convict the world of sin, and of righteousness, and of judgment.' — John 16:8

> ### 'Conviction will produce a godly sorrow and grace that empowers you to repent.'

Conviction is to be found guilty or to be persuaded of truth. Conviction is the invisible aspect of repentance. We can only repent of that which we are convicted of. This is the work of the Holy Spirit and Word of God (John16:8). Conviction is not the same as condemnation. A conviction will produce a godly sorrow and grace that empowers you to repent (2 Corinthians 7:10). It is truth revealed by God. Condemnation is truth without love or hope. This leads to death and destruction. Two examples of this are Peter (conviction) and Judas (condemnation). Peter denied Jesus at His darkest hour but repented and was restored to Christ. Judas also betrayed Jesus and was remorseful, but his sorrow led to his untimely death. Both betrayed Jesus but one was restored to life and the other went to his death.

There are two responses we can choose when God convicts us of sin; acknowledge and respond (Acts 2:37) or ignore and harden your heart (Acts 7:54). The difference is a matter of pride vs. humility. See the scripture below:

'My son, do not despise the chastening of the Lord, Nor detest His correction; For whom the Lord loves He corrects, just as a father the son in whom he delights.' — Proverbs 3:11-12

How do you respond to conviction? Just how we respond will determine if we are God's children. God is our Father and uses the conviction of the Holy Spirit to correct us. He must correct us as His children. In Hebrews, Paul teaches that we should not despise the correction that Father God gives us as His children. Correction however, is not rejection. It protects our relationship with God and perfects Christ-like character within us, that we can relate to Him as Father and bear the fruit of righteousness (Hebrews 12:5-11). Do not despise correction by ignoring the conviction He brings to your heart; humble yourself and respond to the truth of God's Word and Holy Spirit. He resists the proud but will give grace to the humble.

Confession

> *'If we confess our sins, He is faithful and just to forgive us our sins and to cleanse us from all unrighteousness.'* — 1 John 1:9

The second aspect of repentance is confession. Confession is the vocal part of repentance. The word confess means 'to agree with'. Although God knows and sees everything, we demonstrate that we recognise that He does by confessing to Him in the place of prayer.

In the scripture above we can see three key points; God's promises, God's condition and God's character. First, God's promises in the above verse are forgiveness and cleansing. Forgiveness is to be delivered from the penalty of sin or freed from the consequences of disobedience. Cleansing deals with the removal of guilt and shame in your conscience and innocence being restored (justification).

The second point is God's condition. We will only experience God's promise of forgiveness and cleansing if we meet His condition of confession. Confession will produce real and sincere prayer from a heart of humility. Sometimes we can tell God what we think He wants to hear. We can offer religious and ceremonial prayers, but this is not what real intimacy is about. A sign of real intimacy is transparency. The Bible says that Adam and Eve were 'naked and not ashamed' (Genesis 2:24). This 'nakedness' is also symbolic of being open and honest in your heart with the one you are in a relationship with. For intimacy to be maintained in any relationship, both parties must be transparent in communication, especially if one has wronged the other.

Is there any danger in having unconfessed sin? The answer is simply yes. In Proverbs 28:13, it says 'He who covers his sins will not prosper, but whoever confesses and forsakes them will have mercy.' The word 'prosper' means to 'push forward, be profitable or be good'. This means you cannot move forward with a heart full of unconfessed sins! When issues are not confessed or confronted in friendships, marriages or within families, then barriers are created which prevent relationships from flourishing in love and

> *'Confession requires us to speak our prayers to the Lord and not just think them in our mind.'*

freedom. For the barriers to be removed and the relationship to be restored once again, there must be confession (James 5:16). This is the same with our Heavenly Father. Confessing and forsaking sin will restore you to fellowship with God. Not only that but it will maintain fellowship with God. Do not let unconfessed sin cost you your eternity and intimacy with Jesus.

Tell God the convictions in your heart. Be REAL, be SINCERE and be HONEST! Only then can you experience the saving grace of God and the power of the blood of Jesus. It is only the blood of Jesus that can make forgiveness and cleansing possible (Hebrews 9:14). Confession requires us to speak our prayers to the Lord and not just think them in our mind. It is a humbling experience when we hear the words of our heart when speaking to the Lord. However, confession requires the issues to come out from the darkest places of the heart and into the light of God's presence (John 3:20). Talk to Him and experience the liberty and blessing of mercy and forgiveness.

The third point is God's character. In 1 John 1:9 He it describes God as 'faithful and just'. Faithful defines His consistency and 'just' indicates His impartiality and inability to discriminate. If we confess in sincerity and faith, He is FAITHFUL and JUST in His character to forgive. Neither sin nor sinner intimidates God. He made a provision for your position. We can experience the Grace of God and cleansing power of Jesus' Blood when we confess the things the Holy Spirit convicts us of in prayer, as well as to one another.

Restitution

> *'Then Zacchaeus stood and said to the Lord, 'Look, Lord, I give half of my goods to the poor; and if I have taken anything from anyone by false accusation, I restore fourfold.' And Jesus said to him, 'Today salvation has come to this house, because he also is a son of Abraham; for the Son of Man has come to seek and to save that which was lost.' — Luke 19:8-10*

Restitution means 'to give back to the rightful owner' (Exodus 22:6, Leviticus 5:14-19). It is the physical or visible part of repentance. We see an example of restitution when Zacchaeus came to trust in Christ for salvation; he was repentant of his previous wrongs and sought to give back to the rightful owners. He even restored fourfold! The physical change of action and direction is the result of a changed heart and mind. Have a look at the scripture below:

'Or do you not know that your body is the temple of the Holy Spirit who is in you, whom you have from God, and you are not your own? For you were bought at a price; therefore glorify God in your body and in your spirit, which are God's' — 1 Corinthians 6:19-20

> **'Living for Jesus is the highest expression of repentance.'**

We were bought at a price; the precious blood of Jesus. This means our owner is God and He has rightful claim because He is Lord (owner) of all (Psalm 24:1). The sign of repentance is that we give our lives back to God, the rightful owner. Romans 12:1 says 'by the mercies of God, that you present your bodies a living sacrifice, holy, acceptable to God, which is your reasonable service.' It is the mercy of God that causes us to surrender to Him. When God's mercy is revealed to us through the Gospel of Jesus, our reasonable response is to submit to God; spirit, soul and body. Living for Jesus is the highest expression of repentance.

CONCLUSION

The message of repentance is not one of condemnation but restoration. Repentance makes us candidates of the grace that is found in Jesus. It is the key through which we enter into God's provision. Repentance is for saints as well as sinners. Sinners are brought into salvation when they repent and saints remain in fellowship with God through repentance.

Do you need to put things right with God? Do you have any unconfessed sins in your life? Maybe you need to humble yourself by coming to Jesus? If yes, then understand that only through repentance can you be helped by God and refreshed by His presence. Do not hesitate or let pride hinder you from receiving all that God has for you. He gives grace to the humble. Do not harden your heart. Humble yourself before God and experience the blessings of forgiveness and cleansing that is found in Jesus.

'The Lord is not slack concerning His promise, as some count slackness, but is longsuffering toward us, not willing that any should perish but that all should come to repentance.' —
2 Peter 3:9

'Repent therefore and be converted, that your sins may be blotted out, so that times of refreshing may come from the presence of the Lord,' — *Acts 3:19*

CHAPTER 2 — REPENTANCE: PERSONAL STUDY

1. What does repentance mean and which two things does it involve?

   _____

   _____

   _____

   _____

2. Memorise 2 Peter 3:9

3. According to the following verses, what are some of the benefits of repentance? (1 John 1:9, James 5:16, Matthew 4:17, Acts 3:19)

   _____

   _____

   _____

   _____

4. What three stages are involved in biblical repentance? Define them in your own words.

   _____

   _____

   _____

   _____

5. (Exercise) Read 1 John 1:9 and James 5:16. Ask the Holy Spirit to reveal any unconfessed sins in your life and then write them down below or in a notebook. After you have done this, ask for God's mercy and forgiveness in these areas. By faith, thank God that as you confessed, He has forgiven and cleansed you.

   _____

   _____

   _____

   _____

CHAPTER 3: FAITH

'The just shall live by his faith" — Habakkuk 2:4

INTRODUCTION

God has invited us to live by faith. Faith is not reserved for a handful of celebrity Christians who have a unique talent for believing in God. No. All of God's children are called to live by faith. Only by faith, can we live as new creations in Jesus Christ and inherit all that God intends for us. What is faith? What are the characteristics of faith? Will our faith in God be tested? Is faith rewarded? This chapter will focus on answering these questions as we explore biblical faith.

WHAT IS FAITH?

'Faith is a divine confidence in God that produces word of trust and actions of obedience'

The Greek word for faith is 'Pistis' which means, confidence, persuasion, trust, belief or conviction. Faith is a divine confidence in God that produces words of trust and actions of obedience. Faith is the pipeline that transfers the supernatural provision of God into the natural realm. Faith enables the invisible to be brought into the visible. We cannot however generate our faith; it is produced by the word of God (Romans 10:17). God's word generates faith. Trusting in yourself produces arrogance but trusting in God produces divine confidence.

This faith in God will produce a reliance on Christ for salvation and a life that reflects His character (1 John 2:6). Have a look at the following scripture:

> *'Now when Jesus had entered Capernaum, a centurion came*
> *to Him, pleading with Him, saying, 'Lord, my servant is lying*

at home paralyzed, dreadfully tormented.' And Jesus said to him, 'I will come and heal him.'

The centurion answered and said, 'Lord, I am not worthy that you should come under my roof. But only speak a word, and my servant will be healed. For I also am a man under authority, having soldiers under me. And I say to this one, 'Go,' and he goes; and to another, 'Come,' and he comes; and to my servant, 'Do this,' and he does it.' When Jesus heard it, He marvelled, and said to those who followed, 'Assuredly, I say to you, I have not found such great faith, not even in Israel! And I say to you that many will come from east and west, and sit down with Abraham, Isaac, and Jacob in the kingdom of heaven. But the sons of the kingdom will be cast out into outer darkness. There will be weeping and gnashing of teeth.' Then Jesus said to the centurion, 'Go your way; and as you have believed, so let it be done for you.' And his servant was healed that same hour.' — Matthew 8:5-13

The Roman Empire functioned as men under a chain of command. The centurion was an officer under authority. He knew that when he gave a command to those under his authority, his word came with the power and resources to complete the task — regardless of time or distance. He recognised that Christ had absolute authority and saw that God's kingdom operated upon the same principles. His trust in God was founded on these kingdom principles. Though he was not religious, he could see how the Kingdom of God functioned by looking at Jesus. This amazed Jesus, who called it 'great faith!'

Great faith is to understand God's authority. It is recognising the authority of Jesus Christ and responding righteously based upon this knowledge. God is not surprised by anything but great faith. We cannot generate our faith. The Word of God produces the God kind of faith. Faith in God comes by hearing His word and when Jesus is revealed to us by the Holy Spirit (Romans 10:17). Whatever you believe in you access the power of. For example, if you trust in a chair and sit down on it, you access the chair's power to uphold your weight. However, if you trust in God, you access His saving power, eternal life and righteousness. Trusting in yourself will produce arrogance but trusting in God will produce a divine confidence in God. Faith is not a talent reserved to celebrity Christians; it is reliance on Christ through the power of the Holy Spirit.

WHAT IS THE AUTHORITY OF CHRIST?

The Word of God is the absolute authority in the entire universe and beyond. All things were made through God's Word (Hebrews 1:1-3, John 1:1-2). God gave His written word to His children on Mount Sinai. God's written Word pointed to God's Living Word — Jesus Christ. In fact, it was Moses (the Law) and Elijah (the Prophets) that bore witness

> *'It was God's written Word that pointed to God's living Word – Jesus Christ'*

that Jesus is the Fullness of God. In addition, 1 John 5:7 says there are 'three that bear witness in heaven: the Father, the Word, and the Holy Spirit; and these three are one.' Christ Jesus is the Living Word in Heaven that became flesh and dwelt among us on Earth. He then was declared to be the Son of God with power when God raised Him from the dead.

Jesus did not enter into Heaven because of his divine right as God's son. He entered into Heaven through obedience to the Father. Jesus fulfilled complete obedience, so God declared Him the Son of God by raising Him from the dead. He is now the author of eternal salvation to those who obey Him (Hebrews 5:9). The fullness of the Godhead dwells in Jesus (Colossians 2:9). Christ is the living Word of God. He is that same Word that was there in the beginning and He upholds the entire universe. We inherit the reward of Christ's obedience when we put our faith in Him.

> *'And Jesus came and spoke to them, saying, 'All authority has been given to me in heaven and on earth. Go therefore and make disciples of all the nations, baptizing them in the name of the Father and of the Son and of the Holy Spirit, teaching them to observe all things that I have commanded you; and lo, I am with you always, even to the end of the age.' Amen' —*
> *Matthew 28:18-20*

Before Christ told His disciples to 'GO' He gave them a reason; 'All authority has been given to me in heaven and on earth.' Christ Jesus — the Living Word of God, the Son of God has all authority in Heaven, Earth and the underworld. His command was justified because He has all authority! No demon in hell can stop the Gospel because it is packed with God's authority! With Christ's command to 'Go and make disciples' also comes His authority in Heaven, Earth and under the earth! In fact, The Gospel of Jesus Christ brings men under the authority of God. We as believers are now walking in the nature and authority of Jesus Christ the Son of God! As He is so are we!

WHAT IS THE SIGNIFICANCE OF FAITH, HOPE AND LOVE?

1 Corinthians 13:13 says 'And now abide faith, hope, love, these three; but the greatest of these is love.' For you to abide in these three it is important to understand their importance. Just as a fire must have fuel, heat and oxygen so also must we have faith, hope and love to walk in God's perfect will. Let us have a look at the descriptions below.

Hope — The Expectation

Hope is an expectation in which you place your trust. The Bible teaches that hope is the anchor of the soul (Hebrews 6:13). This explains why the soul can become sick or depressed when their hope is not fulfilled (Proverbs 13:12). Everyone must know WHOM he or she believes and WHAT he or she believes them for. As saints, we have a living Hope in Jesus Christ who will raise us from the dead (1 Timothy 1:1, 1 Peter 1:1).

Faith — For Activation

The Bible defines faith as a substance. When we receive knowledge of our Hope, the substance of faith is produced. This is why the Word of God is a key source of faith. Faith cannot go beyond a question mark; neither can it be founded on ignorance. Pick up the bible with unbelief and by the time you finish reading it, you will put it down as a believer. Faith is tangible. Faith is conviction of the truth in God's word. Faith brings Hope into reality. Faith activates the supernatural. Faith is now! Faith transfers our future hope into our present reality.

Love — The Motivation

Love is the inspiration and motivation of our faith. Love is the most sincere and pure motivation of our faith. The Holy Spirit (Romans 5:5) produces this God kind of love within us. Love is perfected in our lives when obedience is fulfilled. In 1 Corinthians 13:3, it says 'Though I bestow all my goods to feed the poor, and though I give my body to be burned, but have not love, it profits me nothing.' This simply means faith should not operate independently to love.

WHAT ARE THE CHARACTERISTICS OF FAITH?

1. Spiritual Law

> *'Where is boasting then? It is excluded. By what law? Of works? No, but by the law of faith.'* — Romans 3:27

Faith is a spiritual law in God's Kingdom. A law is 'a rule of conduct or procedure recognised by a community as binding or enforceable by authority'. A law can also refer to a principle that is predictable. We are citizens on earth but also citizens of the Kingdom of Heaven. As citizens on earth, we have laws that change depending on our country of residence. If you are in England, the laws are limited to working only within the boundaries of England. If you are in America, there are laws that are limited to the boundaries of America. However, as citizens of God's kingdom, we must know that His laws are not limited to any particular country because the earth itself is the Lord's (Psalm 24:1). In fact, God's authority and law extends throughout the universe. This means that as citizens of Heaven we can act by God's law of faith and see the same results every time and anywhere!

2. Joins you to Christ's Identity

> *'For you are all sons of God through faith in Christ Jesus.'* — Galatians 3:26

Faith in Christ Jesus joins us to our identity — Sons of God. Identity is your authority. Identity affects your access to places. Who you are (Identity) inspires what you can do (function). In Matthew 3:17 it says that before Jesus did any major activity the Father declared: 'This is my beloved Son, in whom I am well pleased.' Then after a period of time when His identity was tested in the

'Jesus' activity was the fruit BUT His identity was the root'

wilderness, He then came out and began to preach the Gospel of the Kingdom; casting out demons and healing the sick. This teaches us that His identity was the foundation of His activities. Jesus' activity was the fruit BUT His identity was the root. He was not carrying out activities to become a Son; He was doing His Fathers' work because He is His Son. This is the same for us. We do not work for righteousness; we work from righteousness! Adam sinned and lost the image, but Christ restored the image of God to us. Jesus is the image of God and once we put our faith in Him we are recreated into the image of Christ (Ephesians 2:10). Our security is in Sonship.

John G. Lake said 'in Christ we become God's sons, man's servants and the Devil's masters.' All creation obeyed Adam because he was created in the image of God. What Adam lost because of sin, we have gained through faith in Christ. Jesus is 'the image of the invisible God, the firstborn over all creation' (Colossians 1:15). His image is restored to us through faith. In Christ we are a new creation; we no longer resemble the image of sin but the image of the Lord Jesus Christ (2 Corinthians 5:17).

3. Christ's authority & power

> *'Behold, I give you the authority to trample on serpents and scorpions, and over all the power of the enemy, and nothing shall by any means hurt you. Nevertheless, do not rejoice in this, that the spirits are subject to you, but rather rejoice because your names are written in heaven.' Luke 10:19-20*

The word authority in the verse above comes from the Greek word 'exousia' which means delegated influence, the right to command, jurisdiction or the power given by another. The verse above says that Christ has given us the authority to subdue the 'power' of the enemy. The devil has ability but no legal authority. In Christ, we have the right to command 'all the power of the enemy.' We have been given authority over the devil and ALL his ability.

'Jesus has given us right over the enemies might.'

Jesus has given us right over the enemies' might. There are many things that the Bible says we have authority over; have a look at the list below:

Authority over sickness — Jesus gave His disciples power to heal sickness (Mark 3:15-16). As God's children, we no longer need to talk to God about the disease, because we have received authority to command the disease to go in Jesus' name! 1 John 3:8 says *'For this purpose the Son of God was manifested, that He might destroy the works of the devil.'* Sicknesses and disease are works of the devil. They did not originate in Heaven and it is not God's will for you to be sick. Jesus healed the sick in His earthly ministry and then transferred His authority to us before He ascended into Heaven. You have authority to command sickness so tell it where to go!

Authority over sin — Romans 6:14 says 'for *sin shall not have dominion over you, for you are not under law but under grace.'* The word 'grace' is *'Charis'* in Greek, which is the divine ability of God. Grace is a divine empowerment from God that enables you to live like Jesus Christ. When we are under Jesus' authority then we receive His grace to reign over the sinful nature. Faith in Christ connects us to His victory over sin.

Authority over Satan — As we have mentioned earlier Jesus said in Luke 10:19 *'I give you the authority to trample on serpents and scorpions, and over all the power of the enemy, and nothing shall by any means hurt you.'* Satan and every evil spirit are now subject to us through Christ Jesus. Unfortunately, some Christians shout at God and only whisper at the devil. This should not be so. There is a time to talk with God but there is a time to command the devil in Jesus' name! We have also received authority to free those bound by the devil in Jesus' name!

4. Gives God's perspective: Victory!

'For whatever is born of God overcomes the world. And this is the victory that has overcome the world—our faith. Who is he who overcomes the world, but he who believes that Jesus is the Son of God?" — 1 John 5:4-5

The word 'overcome' comes from the Greek word *'Nike'* which means subdue, prevail, conquer or get the victory. The world is not a playground but a battlefield. Faith is a fight. Nevertheless, we do not fight for victory; we fight from the place of victory. Victory is a position that we have inherited through Christ Jesus. It is also a disposition — a perspective, attitude and a way of thinking. God cannot lose, nor can He be defeated. Therefore, we cannot lose or be defeated. The victory that Christ won on

The Cross is transferred to us by grace; we then enforce it by faith! Even when we experience trials, we can trust that it is working out for our good because we have been called for God's purpose (Romans 8:28). Because He lives, we live also. We cannot lose because He did not lose. Faith in Christ produces a perspective of victory!

> **'We do not fight for victory; we fight from the place of victory.'**

5. Faith and forgiveness

'Judge not, and you shall not be judged. Condemn not, and you shall not be condemned. Forgive, and you will be forgiven.' — Luke 6:37

'Take heed to yourselves. If your brother sins against you, rebuke him; and if he repents, forgive him. And if he sins against you seven times in a day, and seven times in a day returns to you, saying, 'I repent,' you shall forgive him.' And the apostles said to the Lord, 'Increase our faith.' — Luke 17:3-5

The word 'forgive' comes from the Greek word 'aphesis' which means a sending away, a letting go, a release, pardon or complete forgiveness. Forgiveness is to let go of an offense, pardon a crime and to cancel a debt. In Matthew 18:22-35 Jesus uses a parable of a king settling accounts with his servants to explain the concept of forgiveness to us. The king pardons the servant's debt because he begged him, however when the servant that received a pardon from the king went out, he would not pardon the debt of his fellow servant. Because of this the king reinstated that servant's original debt. This parable shows us two things — God's promise and God's condition. With God's promise, the parable explains that God pardons our sins when we put our faith in Jesus. God's condition is that He will only forgive us if we forgive the wrongs of others. In fact in Matthew 6:12 Jesus told us to pray *'And forgive us our debts, AS we forgive our debtors.'* This teaches us that the mercy we receive from God is directly dependent upon the mercy and forgiveness we give to others.

A debt owed may not be money. Sometimes people can owe you an apology, items, or even respect. It causes pain and leads to an offense, which separates the relationship. Sometimes the relationship can continue, but there is a distance or withdrawal of intimacy. Forgiveness does not promise a change in the person's behaviour but it does promise a change in your heart. Are you offended? Faith in the love of God will enable us to forgive others. Forgiveness towards others is a sign of faith towards God. Faith in Jesus forgiving you for all of the things you did to God will inspire you to humble yourself and forgive others.

> 'Therefore I say to you, her sins, which are many, are forgiven, for she loved much. But to whom little is forgiven, the same loves little.' — Luke 7:47

6. Faith is a shield of protection

> 'Above all, taking the shield of faith with which you will be able to quench all the fiery darts of the wicked one.' — Ephesians 6:16

Faith in God protects your heart and mind from spiritual opposition. The word 'shield' in the verse above refers to a large door type shield known as The Scutum. It was light enough to hold in one hand and its large height and width covered the entire soldier. This made it very unlikely for him to be struck during missile fire and in hand-to-hand combat. The shield's size also gave the soldier confidence in battle. As Christians, we must understand that our battle is very real and very close. Our enemy does not use tangible weapons such as a sword or shield but fiery arrows of lies, doubt and temptation. Psalm 18:30 says '*As for God, His way is perfect; the word of the Lord is proven; He is a shield to all who trust in Him.*' It is what our faith connects to that will be our shield — God Himself! When we put our faith in Him, He becomes our shield! He is our protection and as we trust in Him, His presence and Word protects our heart from the arrows of accusations, lies and doubts the enemy sends — praise God!

7. Faith brings peace and spiritual rest

> 'Therefore, having been justified by faith, we have peace with God through our Lord Jesus Christ,' — Romans 5:1

Faith in Jesus produces peace. In John 14:27 Jesus said '*Peace I leave with you, my peace I give to you; not as the world gives do I give to you. Let not your heart be troubled, neither let it be afraid.*' We receive a supernatural peace when we trust in Jesus. It is something the world cannot offer you. In the world, you can be offered prescriptions to sooth anxiety. This does not deal with the root issue. Jesus however brings complete rest of soul when you come to Him (Matthew 11:28). His peace does not mean the absence of trials, but an assurance of His comfort. In John 19:20 Jesus said on The Cross 3 very profound words, *'it is finished.'* When we trust in Him, we can rest in the finished work of The Cross. The reality however, is that many Christians do not know what the true riches are. The devil looks to steal valuable things, but this is not primarily just money or jewellery. Peace is one of the riches God has given us through Christ.

Read on for a guide on how you can maintain the peace God has given you.

HOW DO YOU MAINTAIN PEACE?

'Be anxious for nothing, but in everything by prayer and supplication, with thanksgiving, let your requests be made known to God; and the peace of God, which surpasses all understanding, will guard your hearts and minds through Christ Jesus.' — Philippians 4:6-7

It is amazing that when looking at the verse above it seems like just an exhortation at first glance, but after another look, the Holy Spirit reveals a fantastic guideline for maintaining the peace of God in our hearts. Have a look at these 3 points and may His peace guard you and guide you.

Have zero tolerance for anxiety!

By definition, anxiety is 'a feeling of worry, nervousness, or unease about something with an uncertainty of its outcome.' Anxiety is the seed of depression, hopelessness, and despair (Proverbs 12:25). If we entertain any thought that brings anxiety, we are allowing for a potential forest of hopelessness to grow in our hearts and manifest in our lives (Mark 4:18-19). Choose not to harbour such thoughts or feelings in your mind and heart by acknowledging them as soon as they emerge. 'Be anxious about NOTHING!'

Turn ALL cares into prayers!

You can never be full of Christ until you are empty of yourself. The Bible says in 1 Peter 5:5-7 that we should cast our cares on Him BECAUSE he cares for us! It will insult God's love and desire for you if you think He does not care about everything about you (Matthew 10:10, Zechariah 2:8). In a relationship, transparency is the proof of authentic intimacy (Genesis 2:25). We show God we trust Him when we bring our heart and its contents to Him with honesty and thanksgiving in prayer (Proverbs 3:5-6).

> *'In a relationship transparency is the proof of authentic intimacy.'*

When we give our cares to God, our heart is then open for Him to share His heart and cares to us – when we read the Bible, in prayer and while we go throughout our day.

Let God's peace be your compass!

Incomprehensible peace floods our hearts when we have truly given things over to Him. We do not stop spending time with God in prayer until we are tired or have run out of things to say. No. We finish when there is peace! God's peace guides you as it is a sign of His promise (John 14:27). Peace guards your heart against anxiety and worry that chokes the life out of your faith (Philippians 4:6-7). However, encountering His peace does not mean you should rush out of prayer and fellowship with God; it may be time to be still and just listen! For God speaks in the place of peace and stillness (1 Kings 19:12, Psalm 46:10). In 1 Peter 5:6-7 it says *'Humble yourselves, therefore, under God's mighty hand, that he may lift you up in due time. Cast all your anxiety on him because he cares for you.'* Access God's peace in your life by casting all your cares on Him and maintain God's peace by continuing to do so.

WHAT ARE THE SIGNS OF FAITH?

There is a multitude of signs of authentic biblical faith. Listed below are some key signs of what the God kind of faith looks like:

Actions of obedience

> 'You see then that a man is justified by works, and not by faith
> only.' — James 2: 24

Actions are the sign of living faith. In James 2 we understand that Abraham was justified when he offered his son Isaac. His faith in God produced works or action. Abraham's faith was made perfect by actions. This only means that the result of faith is actions of obedience to God. Faith is revealed in works of righteousness, therefore without actions, there cannot be living faith (Hebrews 4:2).

Words of command

> '....if you have faith as a mustard seed, you will say to this
> mountain, 'Move from here to there,' and it will move; and
> nothing will be impossible for you.' Matthew 17:20

It is amazing that Jesus said if we have faith then we would speak to mountains. There is a time when we are to talk to God, but there is a time when we

'Faith in God gives you His authority to command creation.'

must speak to creation. Faith in God gives you His authority to command creation. Just as Adam had the power to name the things God placed in front of him; so do we (Genesis 2:19). A minister once said 'The Word of God in our mouth is the same as the Word of God spoken in His mouth.' When we speak the Word of faith to things around us, they will respond to the authority of God as if He Himself is speaking.

Confidence and thanksgiving in prayer

> 'Therefore I say to you, whatever things you ask when you
> pray, believe that you receive them, and you will have
> them.' — Mark 11:24,

What do you do when you have received something? You say thank you. Thanksgiving is the result of authentic faith. When you ask, God says *'whatever things you ask when you pray, believe that you receive them, and you will have them.'*

Personally, I have seen and know this to be true. A student sent me a message asking for my help to receive the baptism of the Holy Spirit. He said he had been seeking this for years and knew its significance from what he read in the Bible. After few minutes of talking, I said, 'talk to God as if you have already received Him.' As he began to pray and then thank God with me, it took only a few moments before the fire of God ignited His heart and he irrupted in tongues! He was flat out on the floor in his University Lecture Theatre for over two hours worshiping and praying! Faith thanks God in advance and produces an attitude of thanksgiving.

Faith is to thank God in advance in the natural for what He has already done in the spiritual realm. It is from a position of thanksgiving that we receive in the natural the provision that God has the spirit! In 1 John 5:14 it says:

> *'Now this is the confidence that we have in Him, that if we ask anything according to His will, He hears us.'*

Trust in God produces confidence in God. This kind of confidence is not self-generated but inspired by His Word and Holy Spirit. This God kind of confidence is humility. Trusting in your ability alone will produce arrogance. This is not faith because the source of strength is yourself and not God. God rewards confidence (Hebrews 10:53). Confidence is produced when we know the will of God in all aspects of our lives. We can have confidence in God because we know His desire and can pray according to His will. The word of God reveals the will of God.

Supernatural vision

'For we walk by faith, not by sight.' Two Corinthians 5:7

The opposite of faith is not fear; the opposite of faith is sight. This is because the five senses can inspire doubt, which leads to fear. The word of God states a reality that is usually the complete opposite of what you see around you. However, faith enables you to see God's truth, regardless of what the natural circumstances show you.

WILL FAITH BE TESTED?

In this you greatly rejoice, though now for a little while, if need be, you have been grieved by various trials, that the genuineness of your faith, being much more precious than gold that perishes, though it is tested by fire, may be found to praise, honour, and glory at the revelation of Jesus Christ, whom having not seen you love. Though now you do not see Him, yet believing, you rejoice with joy inexpressible and full of glory,' — 1 Peter 1:6-8

Your faith will be tested! There is a difference between when God is testing us and when the devil is tempting us. The testing or temptation of the devil is to lead a person into sin. The testing of God is to reveal the authenticity of our trust in Him. One of the key things we can learn from the verse above is that it is not a matter of what trial we face but the quality of faith that was produced

> *'The testing of God is to reveal the authenticity of our trust in Him.'*

through the process. Peter compares the testing of faith to gold purified in fire. Just as the purpose of the fire is to remove impurity that produces pure and authentic gold, so are trials meant to reveal the worth and authenticity of our faith in God. Trials should not be despised but understood (Hebrews 5:8). Here are three ways our faith can be tested:

Time — Can your faith stand the test of time? Faith in God brings immediate results. However, some of His promises are fulfilled over a period of time. His time and NOT our time. An example of this test was in the life of Abraham. The Lord gave him a promise concerning a child but did not immediately indicate when the child was to be born. The story of Abraham teaches us that God may not give you all the details when He leads you. However when we act in faith and obedience we can be sure that He will bring us to His expected end. Nothing tests faith more than time. Patience is when faith in God continues over time (see Genesis 12-22).

Truth — The truth of God's word tests our faith in Him. When we read the word of God, we receive faith in God. The word of God does not only generate faith, but it also determines what authentic faith looks like. It is the framework to measure if our faith is authentic. In John 7:38 Jesus says:

'He who believes in me, <u>as the Scripture</u> has said, out of his heart will flow rivers of living water.' It is only faith that is according to scripture that will experience the overflow of the Holy Spirit. Society and opinion have tried to customize faith in God to meet their opinion or satisfy their pleasures. However, God has stated that there is only one authentic faith that He responds to (Ephesians 4:8). This faith pleases God and He has revealed the principles and pattern of faith for us to follow in His word (Romans 4). Faith in God must line up to and be tested by scripture.

Trials — A trial is a challenging experience or difficult period we will go through in our Christian journey. The Bible says that when you go through this, you should be joyful because patience is being produced as your faith is tested (James 1:3). Trials teach us to trust in the consistency of God's character rather than the changing nature of our circumstances. Job learned this when his faith was being tested. As we become patient (constant in character), we develop the same consistency in our character as God, no matter the circumstances.

CONCLUSION

'But without faith it is impossible to please Him, for he who comes to God must believe that He is, and that He is rewarded of those who diligently seek Him.' — Hebrews 11:6

How do you approach God? Do you approach in belief or unbelief? Sometimes people once trusted in God but things did not happen as they expected. They then become discouraged and hurt from a negative experience and feel reluctant to trust in God again. However, the Bible says in 2 Corinthians 5:17 *'all things have become new.'* God can renew your faith, heal your heart and restore your expectations, as you trust in Jesus again.

Everyone must know WHOM he or she believes and WHAT he or she believes them for. In 1 Peter 1:21 it says *'through Him believe in God, who raised Him from the dead and gave Him glory so that your faith and hope are in God.'* Have you put your faith in Jesus? It pleased God to raise Jesus from the dead and it pleases God that we put our faith in Jesus. Turn to Jesus and live a life of faith in Him, *'receiving the end of your faith—the salvation of your souls.' — 1 Peter 1:9.*

CHAPTER 3 — FAITH: PERSONAL STUDY

1. Read Matthew 8:5-13. What is faith and how does it relate to understanding authority?

    _____

    _____

    _____

2. Reflect on the seven characteristics of faith mentioned earlier in this chapter. How can you apply them practically in your life?

    _____

    _____

    _____

3. According to Philippians 4:6-7, what 3 actions can you take to access and maintain God´s peace?

    _____

    _____

    _____

4. According to James 2, what makes faith perfect?

    _____

    _____

    _____

5. Exercise. As faith is a shield of protection, write all the negative words or excuses that sow seeds of doubt and fear in your mind. After you have done this, next to each statement find a bible promise you can use to guard your heart with. For example, 'I can't do it' — Bible verse — Philippians 4:13

    _____

    _____

    _____

    _____

CHAPTER 4: BAPTISMS

'Repent, and let every one of you be baptized in the name of Jesus Christ for the remission of sins; and you shall receive the gift of the Holy Spirit.' — Acts 2:38

'Buried with Him in baptism, in which you also were raised with Him through faith in the working of God, who raised Him from the dead.' — Colossians 2:12

INTRODUCTION

Baptism is more than just a ritual sprinkling of water or meaningless ceremony. Baptism explains the reality that God has accomplished for us through Christ Jesus- being fully immersed. Full immersion depicts God's desire for full contact with us. What is baptism? What are we baptized into? Are there requirements? As we explore the biblical significance of baptism may you be immersed into God's fullness as you read in Jesus name!

WHAT DOES BAPTISM MEAN?

The Greek word for baptism is 'baptizo', which means to make fully wet, to wash or to fully immerse. Baptism describes the introduction of someone into a new place, or to bring a person into union with something that changes his or her previous state. A person is immersed in water to symbolize complete purification. It can also signify being introduced to a new life or new beginning.

ARE THERE OLD TESTAMENT EXAMPLES OF BAPTISM?

The biblical accounts of salvation through water in the Old Testament were symbolic of God's plan of salvation for His people in the New Testament Gospel. Here are some examples of water baptism in the Old Testament.

Noah

> '....in the days of Noah, while the ark was being prepared, in
> which a few, that is, eight souls, were saved through water.
> There is also an antitype which now saves us—baptism (not
> the removal of the filth of the flesh, but the answer of a good
> conscience toward God), through the resurrection of Jesus
> Christ," — 1 Peter 3:20-21

God saved Noah through the water. God instructed Noah to build an ark that would be used to save his family from a great flood. The same water that brought destruction to the earth was also used for Noah's deliverance. The story of Noah is symbolic of God's people being delivered from the present fallen world and brought into the world that God will give as an inheritance to those who trust in Him — Heaven. The water is symbolic of the transition from our old life and introduction to a new life in Christ Jesus. The story of Noah is a picture of the return of Christ (Matthew 24:37). Those who believe and are baptised demonstrate they are ready for His return.

Moses

> 'All were baptized into Moses in the cloud and in the sea' —
> 1 Corinthians 10:2

God appointed Moses to deliver the children of Israel out of the bondage of Pharaoh, the king of Egypt. Israel trusted in Moses as God's appointed saviour who delivered them from the bondage of Egypt through the water of the Red Sea (Exodus 14:21-31). In 1 Corinthians 10:1-4 it says that the Israelites were 'baptized into Moses in the cloud and the sea.' This means that they were unified with him in the transition from slavery to freedom and from death to a new life. As well as the blood of the Passover lamb, the symbol of their departure was following Moses through the water. This story is also symbolic of baptism and has direct application today. Now for us, the symbol of our transition from the bondage of the devil and transition into freedom is that we trust God's appointed servant Jesus and are baptized with water in His name.

Naaman

'And Elisha sent a messenger to him, saying: 'Go and wash in the Jordan seven times, and your flesh shall be restored to you, and you shall be clean.' — 2 Kings 5:10.

In spite of his honour and fame, Naaman needed to be cleansed from his leprosy. After hearing the message of healing and restoration from a servant girl from Israel, Naaman was sent to Elisha who commanded him to wash in the Jordan. After humbling himself to the instructions of the man of God, Naaman came out of the water cleansed from his infirmity. This can be applied to us today. Regardless of our prestige and accolades with men, we are still considered unclean in the sight of God because of sin. If we humble ourselves and by faith obey the word given by God through Jesus, our sins will be cleansed and we will be made whole. Naaman being cleansed by dipping himself seven times in the Jordan is symbolic of us being cleansed from sin when we humbly trust in the Gospel of Jesus and are baptized through faith in Him.

WHAT IS THE PURPOSE OF WATER BAPTISM?

The beginning of the Gospel of Jesus Christ, the Son of God. As it is written in the Prophets: 'Behold, I send my messenger before your face, who will prepare your way before you.' 'The voice of one crying in the wilderness: 'Prepare the way of the Lord; Make His paths straight.' 'John came baptizing in the wilderness and preaching a baptism of repentance for the remission of sins.' — Mark 1:1-4

John was the *'voice of one crying in the wilderness'* spoken of in the book of Isaiah (Isaiah 40:3). His ministry was greater than all of the Old Testament prophets because his message was the beginning of the Gospel of Jesus.

> **'Water baptism also signified being identified with the death burial and resurrection of Christ.'**

John preached a message of repentance from sin and turning towards God, which also means the beginning of the Gospel of Jesus is repentance (Matthew 3:11). Those who repented from sin and turned towards God would be baptized in water in the midst of witnesses. Water baptism symbolized a cleansing from sin and introduction to a new life in Christ.

Water baptism also signified being identified with the death burial and resurrection of Christ. See the scripture below:

> 'Therefore we were buried with Him through baptism into death, that just as Christ was raised from the dead by the glory of the Father, even so we also should walk in newness of life. For if we have been united together in the likeness of His death, certainly we also shall be in the likeness of His resurrection," Romans 6:4-5

This means that when Jesus died we died with Him, when Jesus was buried; we were buried with Him, when Jesus rose from the dead, we rose with Him, and when Jesus ascended into Heaven, we ascended with Him. When Jesus was seated, we also were seated with Him! We no longer live, but He lives through us (Galatians 2:20). Water baptism is the outward symbol of this spiritual reality that we have been brought into through faith in Jesus.

Water baptism is a command given by the Lord. Those who believed in the Gospel of Christ were baptized in water as a symbol of obedience. In the book of Acts, we see that all those who believed in the Gospel would be baptized in water to signify this conversion from death to life.

It is necessary to count the cost of following Jesus (Luke 14:27-29). Just as a bride counts the cost of being identified with her bridegroom, so we must count the cost of being identified with Christ. Those who share in His suffering will also share in His glory. Salvation is like marriage; for better or for worse. Those who confess Him before men, He will confess their names before the Father (Matthew 10:32).

IS THERE A REQUIREMENT FOR BAPTISM?

> 'Then Peter said to them 'Repent, and let every one of you be baptized in the name of Jesus Christ for the remission of sins; and you shall receive the gift of the Holy Spirit.' — Acts 2:38.

There is only one requirement before being baptized — repentance from sin and faith in Jesus. The Bible does not give any other requirement. Age, race or gender should not prevent anyone from being baptized. It is a personal decision, which is why it may be honourable to christen children but they must make a personal decision to trust in Jesus and be baptized. Children cannot merely be christened as a symbol of their faith, but they must eventually make a conscious decision to choose to follow Him when of age to do so.

WHAT ARE WE BAPTIZED INTO?

As previously mentioned, baptism describes the introduction of someone into a new place, or to bring a person into union with something that changes his or her previous state. We will now look at what God brings you into union with when you are baptized.

The Name (Fullness) of God

'..Let every one of you be baptized in the name of Jesus Christ for the remission of sins....' — Acts 2:38

As mentioned in Chapter 1, names were given to reveal the identity, purpose, destiny and character of the person that was born. To be baptized into Jesus' name means to be fully immersed into all that He represents — the fullness of God. Colossians 2:9 says *'For in Him dwells all the fullness of the Godhead bodily.'* This means all the names that God revealed to His people in the Old Testament can be summarized in the name of Jesus. He is the fullness and we have been immersed into God's fullness. Proverbs 18:10 says *'The name of the Lord is a strong tower; the righteous run to it and are safe.''* This means His name is a place of safety and shelter by which those who He has made righteous can take refuge.

The body of Christ

'For by one Spirit we were all baptized into one body— whether Jews or Greeks, whether slaves or free—and have all been made to drink into one Spirit.' — 1 Corinthians 12:13

'The church is the family of God and Heavens embassy on Earth.'

The church is not the venue you go to but the very people you belong to. The church is a holy nation that represents God's heart and authority on earth. The church is the family of God and Heaven's embassy on earth. They are called to represent God's authority, reflect God's glory and join in reconciling the world to God through Jesus.

We are baptized into the family of God and brought into union with the body of Christ — the church. The body of Christ is joined to God as well as one another through the Holy Spirit. The only spirit that joins the body of Christ is the Holy Spirit. This also means that no other's spirit is welcomed in the body of Christ. Regardless of our old identity, whether English, black, white, man or woman, we are now citizens of Heaven and immersed into the church — the family of God. A sign of the relationship with God is that you love the church (1 John 5:1-2).

Fire

> *'I indeed baptize you with water unto repentance. He will baptize you with the Holy Spirit and fire.'* — Matthew 3:11

'The fire of the Holy Spirit is not only given for passion but also for purity.'

Jesus will baptize you in the fire of the Holy Spirit. In Hebrews 12:30 it says *'For our God is a consuming fire'*. When we are baptized we are brought into union with the holy fire of God. This holy fire gives you divine passion and power to preach the Gospel. The fire of the Holy Spirit is not only given for passion but also for purity. Purifying our hearts from sin and carnal thinking. God created our hearts to burn with fervent love and zeal for Him and one another. Actually, the very voice of God will set your heart on fire! In Luke 24:32 the disciples said to one another: *'Did not our heart burn within us while He talked with us on the road, and while He opened the Scriptures to us?'* It is an inward charge of God's fire that keeps you in charge to reign in life.

WHAT IS THE PURPOSE OF BAPTISM IN HOLY SPIRIT?

> *'But you shall receive power when the Holy Spirit has come upon you; and you shall be witnesses to Me in Jerusalem, and in all Judea and Samaria, and to the end of the earth.'* — Acts 1:8

'There is absolutely NO substitute for the Holy Spirit.'

Jesus commanded His disciples to wait for the Promise of the Father (Holy Spirit) because He knew it was impossible for them to accomplish His work without Him (Acts 1:1-8). There is NO substitute for the Holy Spirit. Though they may be honourable; no title, no amount of experience, no wife, no husband, no Ph.D., no model, no theology, no connection can be exchanged for His Person.

In 1 Kings 18:24 Elijah said *'Then you call on the name of your gods, and I will call on the name of the Lord; and the God who answers by fire, He is God.'* The fire was a sign that the offerings people brought were acceptable to God. It was a confirmation that God was pleased with the offering. On the day of Pentecost, God revealed that the acceptable offerings for worship had changed from bringing bulls and rams, to making a sacrifice of praise and worship through Jesus. The fire of the Holy Spirit was sent from Heaven to the disciples because Jesus' perfect sacrifice was acceptable to God! He is a necessity and not an accessory.

In 1 John 3:24 it says *'now he who keeps His commandments abides in Him, and He in him. And by this, we know that He abides in us, by the Spirit whom He has given us.'* This teaches us that the Holy Spirit is the sign of our salvation. He is the One that empowers us to live in Jesus by faith. It is the power of the Holy Spirit that keeps us in the faith (1 Peter 1:5). The proof that we have been redeemed with the blood of Jesus is the Holy Spirit dwelling within us. He is the Power of God. There are several benefits of the baptism of the Holy Spirit. Some of which are listed below:

Power to witness— In Acts 1:8 it says: *'you shall receive power when the Holy Spirit has come upon you; and you shall be witnesses'.* One of the first reasons for Holy Spirit baptism is for divine empowerment to be a witness of Jesus. Although Christ gave His disciples authority (exousia) to use His name, they still needed power. The word 'power' comes from the Greek word 'dunamis', which means miracle-working power, violence or might. This power would enable Jesus' disciples to be 'witnesses' which comes from the Greek word 'martyrdom'. Only by the power of the Holy Spirit can you still profess faith in Jesus while being persecuted or put to death.

Spiritual Gifts — In Acts 2:5 it says *'they were all filled with the Holy Spirit and began to speak with other tongues, as the Spirit gave them utterance.'* Holy Spirit baptism accompanied the believer being given spiritual gifts such as prophecy and speaking in tongues. Spiritual gifts are divine empowerments of grace given by the Holy Spirit to enable the saints to do the work of God (see chapter 6).

> *'Boldness is not based upon personality; it is our inheritance through Jesus.'*

Divine Boldness — In Acts 4:31 it says: *'And when they had prayed, the place was shaken where they were assembled; and they were all filled with the Holy Ghost, and they spoke the word of God with boldness.'* — Acts 4:31. In God's kingdom, boldness is not based upon personality; it is our inheritance through Jesus. Boldness is our birthright. It was the power of the Holy Spirit that changed Peter from being intimidated by a small girl, to being bold to preach the Gospel on the day of Pentecost and lead 3000 men to Christ. It was the power of the Holy Spirit that enabled Paul to preach the gospel from city to city while being under intense persecution. Personally, I know that He gives you boldness. I first stood up to share Gods word at the age of 17. I was exited to serve God but nervous about what I was going to say. But after asking God for help and speaking, this boldness and strength came over me and inspiration to speak. Instead of not knowing what to say, I didn't know where to start. The Holy Spirit gives you the boldness of Jesus. No matter what your personality is, when the Spirit of God comes upon you, God's boldness and authority will be seen in you!

WHAT ABOUT THE FRUITS OF THE SPIRIT?

However, the fruit of the Spirit is love, joy, peace, longsuffering, kindness, goodness, faithfulness, gentleness, self-control. Against such, there is no law.' — Galatians 5:22-23

The Holy Spirit produces the character of Christ within us by grace; we then express Christ's character by faith (Philippians 2:13). The fruits of the Holy Spirit reveal the character of Christ and by them; we know that we have a relationship with God. A sign of intimacy with God is the fruits of the Holy Spirit and NOT the gifts. Fruits are cultivated, but gifts although necessary, are given.

CONCLUSION

Have you been baptized? Jesus said in Mark 16:16 *'He who believes and is baptized will be saved.'* Trust in Jesus and be baptized as a physical symbol of your new spiritual reality. Have you experienced Pentecost? What is amazing is Pentecost is not merely a historical day that happened over 2000 years ago to 120 people in an upper room. Pentecost is a promise that God has given to everyone who trusts in Jesus for salvation. Jesus' blood has washed us and restored our position with God; the Holy Spirit has been given so that we can have communion with God on a 24/7 basis. He is the Father's Promise. Be resolute, ask God for the gift of the Holy Spirit, and by faith receive all that God has for you. When the Holy Spirit has come, you can never be the same again!

'For everyone who asks receives and him who seeks finds, and to him who knocks it will be opened. If a son asks for bread from any father among you, will he give him a stone? Alternatively, if he asks for a fish, will he give him a serpent instead of a fish? Or if he asks for an egg, will he offer him a scorpion? If you then, being evil, know how to give good gifts to your children, how much more will your heavenly Father give the Holy Spirit to those who ask Him?' — Luke 11:10-13

CHAPTER 4 — BAPTISMS: PERSONAL STUDY

1. According to Romans 6:5, Colossians 2:12, what is baptism and what is the purpose of water baptism?

   _____

   _____

   _____

   _____

2. According Acts 2:38, 1 Corinthians 10:12, Matthew 3:11; what three things are someone baptized into?

   _____

   _____

   _____

   _____

3. According to the following scriptures, who is the Holy Spirit? What are His Characteristics? What does He do? John 16:5-15, John 15:25-26, Romans 5:5, Ephesians 4:30, Galatians 5:21-22, Romans 8:11-26.

   _____

   _____

   _____

   _____

4. According to the following scriptures, what happened after people received the Holy Spirit baptism? Acts 1:8, Acts 2:1-5, Acts 4:29-30.

   _____

   _____

   _____

   _____

5. Scriptures to remember are Acts 1:8 and Luke 11:10-13. Pray and ask God to be baptized in the Holy Spirit and thank Him by faith (Mark 11:24).

CHAPTER 5: LAYING ON OF HANDS

'..They will lay hands on the sick, and they will recover.' —
Mark 10:10

INTRODUCTION

Throughout the Gospel, we see that some very powerful things took place when people obeyed the Holy Spirit and laid hands on another person by faith. It wasn't simply a ceremonial action and the results that followed demonstrated that some supernatural occurrence must have taken place. What is laying on of hands? What are the reasons for laying hands on a person? As we explore these questions in this chapter, I pray that you would be ignited and provoked, knowing that it is may be our hands but God's power!

WHAT IS LAYING ON OF HANDS?

Laying on of hands is a biblical practice. Laying on hands allows contact for the transmission of God's divine power to flow to another person. When laying hands on a person, a very real and tangible impartation takes place. It is a means by which God releases His supernatural power through our natural hands.

> *'Laying on hands makes contact for the transmission of Gods divine power to flow to another person.'*

The hand can also have a symbolic meaning of power and provision in the Bible. For example, God said He would lay His hand on Egypt in judgment, which brought great displays of His power (Exodus 7:4). Even the apostles asked that God's hand would be stretched out to heal after Pentecost (Acts 4:28-29). There is no power in merely putting your hands on someone, however when done by faith and by God's Word then 'signs' will follow (Mark 16:18). It is not about us but who we are connected to – God almighty. Laying on of hands is when God releases His power and provision to another through the hands of His saints.

WHAT IS THE PURPOSE OF LAYING ON OF HANDS?

There are several different accounts of people laying hands in the bible. Listed below are five different purposes for laying hands on another:

1. Blessing and impartation

> *Then Israel stretched out his right hand and laid it on Ephraim's head, who was the younger, and his left hand on Manasseh's head, guiding his hands knowingly, for Manasseh was the firstborn. And he blessed Joseph, and said: 'God, before whom my fathers Abraham and Isaac walked, The God who has fed me all my life long to this day, The Angel who has redeemed me from all evil, Bless the lads; Let my name be named upon them, and the name of my fathers Abraham and Isaac; And let them grow into a multitude in the midst of the earth.' — Genesis 48:14-16*

'Blessing can involve inviting God's divine help through prayer and the laying on of hands.'

Isaac blessed his son Jacob through the laying on of hands (Genesis 27:27). The Hebrew word for 'bless' is 'Barak' which means divine advantage, help from above, fortunate to be envied, to bless. Blessing can involve inviting God's divine help through prayer and the laying on of hands. The words of blessing that are spoken over the individual reveal the way the blessing of God will manifest in a person's life. When God has blessed a person — they are blessed. Period. In Genesis 48 Israel prayed that the divine provision God had given him would be transferred onto Joseph's children. Similarly, in the New Testament Jesus gathered young children unto Himself and laid His hands on them while pronouncing God's blessing on them (Mark 10:16). This shows that this practice to bless is not reserved for the Old Testament alone. Today we can also pronounce God's blessing on others by prayer and laying hands on them.

When I used to live at home, my mother would put her hands on my brothers and I and pray God's blessing. Although I did not understand it at the time, I can see that the words of God she spoke into my life are happening. I would encourage parents to lay hands on their children and speak words of blessing!

2. Appointment into leadership

> 'And the Lord said to Moses: 'Take Joshua the son of Nun with you, a man in whom is the Spirit, and lay your hand on him; set him before Eleazar, the priest and before all the congregation, and inaugurate him in their sight. And you shall give some of your authority to him, that all the congregation of the children of Israel may be obedient.' —
> Numbers 27:18-20

The authority was transferred from Moses to Joshua to be the next leader of Israel. God commanded Moses to lay his hands on him to 'inaugurate' or 'commission' him in the presence of the congregation. Commissioning describes the authority granted to a person or organization to act as a representative on behalf of another. Joshua was now authorized to judge the people of Israel in place of Moses. The bible says the spirit of wisdom rested upon Joshua from that point onwards. All authority inherently comes from God. However, He can delegate His authority to men for them to represent Him. The authority that Moses transferred to Joshua was therefore God's because He put Moses in authority to lead.

The laying on of hands was used to transfer delegated authority and appoint people into leadership. In another account, God also commanded Moses to lay hands when appointing seventy elders into offices (Numbers 11:16-17). These seventy also followed the same divine pattern when appointing leaders. This same principle was seen in the New Testament when the Apostles appointed seven men to run the churches' business (Acts 6:3-6). Only the one in authority can transfer the power to act on their behalf through the laying on of hands.

Not being hasty

The specific practice of laying hands to appoint people into church offices or leadership positions should not be taken lightly or done hastily. Have a look at the following verse:

'I charge you before God and the Lord Jesus Christ and the elect angels that you observe these things without prejudice, doing nothing with partiality. Do not lay hands on anyone hastily, nor share in other people's sins; keep yourself pure.' — 1 Timothy 5:22

Before laying hands to appoint people into church leadership and office, their character must be recognised and not just their charisma (gifting). 1 Timothy 3:1-3 teaches us that character must be tested to have

'Character must be recognised and not just Charisma.'

confidence that the person can handle the responsibility of leadership. In addition, in Ecclesiastes 7:1 it says *'A good name is better than precious ointment....'* This means it is better to go without anointing than to go without character. Pursue both but do not go without character. I have found this to be true. During the early stages of ministry, I noticed that although God's gift was evidently working in my life, some people would be repelled by my actions and character. As I began to address some of my character flaws with the help of God and mentors, I found the very same people who were previously repelled, began to respond to me in a more respectful and trusting way. Gifts make for ability, character makes for sustainability. If you are going to appoint people into leadership, do not only observe ability and charisma, recognise and test their character!

3. Atonement in Old Testament worship

'Then he shall put his hand on the head of the burnt offering, and it will be accepted on his behalf to make atonement for him.' — Leviticus 1:4

Laying on of hands was used in the Old Testament worship ceremony. The animal would be brought to the brazen altar to be offered to make atonement for the sins of the worshiper. The worshipper would confess all his sins while laying hands on the animal sacrifice. The innocence of the animal would be transferred on to the worshipper temporarily. The guilt of the worshipper would be transferred onto the animal sacrifice. Laying on of hands was also used for the penalty of blasphemy against God (Leviticus 24:13-15). There is no example of laying hands on animals' sacrifice in the New Testament practice. Have a look at the scripture below that explains why:

*'By that will we have been sanctified through the offering of
the body of Jesus Christ once for all? And every priest stands
ministering daily and offering repeatedly the same sacrifices,
which can never take away sins. But this Man, after He had
offered one sacrifice for sins forever, sat down at the right
hand of God,'* — Hebrews 10:10-12

Jesus is the all-sufficient sacrifice offered for our sins. Unlike the Old Testament offerings that couldn't take away our sins, Jesus offered Himself and washed us from our sins in His blood. We no longer need to offer up animals or lay hands on them because our sins have been purged through faith in Jesus! Praise God!

4. Receiving Holy Spirit baptism and spiritual gifts

*'And when Paul had laid hands on them, the Holy Spirit came
upon them, and they spoke with tongues and prophesied'* —
Acts 19:6

In the New Testament, people received the Holy Spirit baptism by the laying on of hands. This would accompany manifestation of spiritual gifts such as speaking in tongues and prophecy. These spiritual gifts can also be imparted by the laying on of hands ((one Timothy 4:14). However laying on of hands was not the only way people received Holy Spirit baptism. At times people were baptized in the Holy Spirit straight after their water baptism and during the preaching of the Word of God (Acts 10:44). This is amazing! This teaches us that laying on of hands is a way in which God can give the Holy Spirit. However, He does not solely rely on hands being laid for a person to receive the Holy Spirit, praise God!

5. Healing the sick

*'And these signs will follow those who believe: In My name
they will cast out demons; they will speak with new tongue...
they will lay hands on the sick, and they will recover.'* — Mark
16:17-18

'It's truly our hands but Gods power!'

God can perform supernatural healing when His people lay hands on the sick. Authority to heal is given to every believer through faith in Jesus. Paul saw the father of Publius healed from a fever after he prayed and laid hands on him (Acts 28:8). The Bible also says that God worked unusual miracles through Paul's hands so that handkerchiefs and aprons from his body were used to heal the sick and cast out demons (Acts 19:12). However laying hands was not the only means that God worked healing. Jesus healed the centurion's servant at a distance simply by speaking a word (Matthew 8:13). This teaches us that God can work miracles by various methods, but acting by faith in obedience to the Holy Spirit is what's key.

I was invited to speak in an outreach in Birmingham UK. After speaking on the love of God, I invited people to come to the front for prayer for healing and restoration. An elderly woman came up to be prayed for healing in her eyes from cataracts. I simply thanked God for being our healer and commanded healing in her eyes in Jesus' name! The woman shook under the power of God and was grateful for my prayer. Within twenty minutes of leaving the café where the outreach was held; I received a message from the woman's daughter, saying that God had completely healed her cataracts! Hallelujah! It is truly our hands but ultimately God's power!

'Signs and wonders follow faith and not position'

Believe God and speak healing with boldness. Believe God and lay hands on the sick with boldness and wonders will follow! You do not need to wait until you have an official church position before God can work healing through your hands. Believe, act and signs will follow. Signs and wonders follow faith and not position. Period.

PRACTICAL GUIDELINES FOR LAYING HANDS

God began to remove my ignorance and break the intimidation with this statement 'our hands, Gods power.' Here is a brief and practical guide for laying hands on people.

1. Identify the need

You can do this by asking the person what they believing God is to do right now. Sometimes people do not want prayer for the obvious reasons. I have seen people on crutches come to receive prayer to pass their exams so do not assume! God gives us spiritual gifts such as words of knowledge to help identify what the needs are for which to pray. In this case, let the Holy Spirit speak to you and then mention what He is revealing to you by faith.

2. Place your hand on the area of the body

In Matthew 9:29 it says *'Then He touched their eyes, saying, 'According to your faith let it be to you.'* Jesus placed His hand directly upon the area of need in order for the power of God to be directly transferred into that part of the body. This is not a set rule because people were healed in various ways (Matthew 8:14, Matthew 15:36), however seek to place your hand on the specific area.

3. Speak healing to the area of the body or issue

In Matthew 17:20 it says *'if you have faith as a mustard seed, you will say to this mountain, 'Move from here to there,' and it will move; and nothing will be impossible for you.'* This tells us that faith in Christ gives you the authority to command things. Thank God for the promise of healing and then command the sickness or issue to go in Jesus' name! By faith see God's love and power flowing through you and into the other person. According to Mark 11:24 thank Him and be expectant for manifestation!

These are simple guidelines to help you get started in praying for people around you. As mentioned earlier, although we should not be hasty in laying hands upon a person to appoint into office, you can lay hands on people for healing and pray for their needs.

CONCLUSION

Some very powerful things take place when people obey the Holy Spirit and lay hands on a person by faith. There are various reasons why you can lay hands on a person. To appoint someone into leadership is reserved to those with delegated authority. However, you do not need to wait until you have an official church position before God can work healing through your hands. Believe, act and signs will follow. Be bold and have confidence in Jesus, remembering that God's power works through our hands.

CHAPTER 5 — LAYING ON OF HANDS: PERSONAL STUDY

1. Write the five purposes for laying hands in the bible? Can you identify any other reasons?

    _____

    _____

    _____

    _____

2. Search the scriptures and give examples of when laying on of hands proceeded healing, commissioning and Holy Spirit baptism.

    _____

    _____

    _____

    _____

3. Why is it important for a person who is laying hands on another person to be living a life of holiness? Write your reflections.

    _____

    _____

    _____

    _____

CHAPTER 6: GIFTS OF THE HOLY SPIRIT

'Pursue love, and desire spiritual gifts....' —
1 Corinthians 14:1

INTRODUCTION

Every follower of Jesus must understand that biblical Christianity is one hundred percent supernatural. As co-labourers of God, we have been given a supernatural 'tool-kit' so that we can collaborate with Jesus in reconciling the world to God — spiritual gifts. Not only was Jesus' Identity transferred to us, but so also was His ministry. We are told not to be ignorant of various key things in the scripture — the afterlife, the devices of the enemy and spiritual gifts (1 Thessalonians 4:13, 2 Corinthians 2:11, 1 Corinthians 12:1). What then are spiritual gifts? Can anyone operate in spiritual gifts? What is the purpose for them? In this chapter, we will look at these questions. I pray that God places within you a holy hunger for spiritual gifts to serve God's church and reach out to the lost world in Jesus' name.

WHAT ARE SPIRITUAL GIFTS?

'For to one is given the word of wisdom through the Spirit, to another the word of knowledge through the same Spirit, to another faith by the same Spirit, to another gifts of healings by the same Spirit, to another the working of miracles, to another prophecy, to another discerning of spirits, to another different kinds of tongues, to another the interpretation of tongues. But one and the same Spirit works all these things, distributing to each one individually as He wills.' —
1 Corinthians 12:8-12

Spiritual gifts are divine empowerments of grace given by the Holy Spirit. They are supernatural abilities that the Holy Spirit gives you to fulfill the great commission Jesus gave to His church. There are many dimensions of

God's grace. One of which is His saving grace, which regenerated us and made us new creations in Christ Jesus. Another aspect is the serving grace by which God's Spirit works through you to reach out to another in order to fulfill His purpose.

The Spirit of God works through spiritual gifts for three main reasons. Firstly to edify and build the church, which is also known as the body of Christ (Ephesians 4:12-13). The second reason is to reveal God's love to those who are non-believers. When the Spirit of God works through spiritual gifts, God's love can be experienced and perceived by both believers and unbelievers alike (1 Corinthians 14:1-40).

> *'Supernatural abilities that the Holy Spirit gives you in order to fulfill the great commission Jesus gave to His church!'*

The third reason spiritual gift are given is to engage in spiritual warfare. Spiritual war is the act of confronting spiritual forces that are opposed to the purpose and plan of God for your life and others. In Ephesians 6:12 it says *'For we do not wrestle against flesh and blood,'* this means our 'wrestle' is never with people, even if they may be used by the enemy. We cannot fight spiritual battles with physical weapons. Paul encouraged Timothy to use the prophecies he received to wage warfare (1Timoty 1:18). This teaches us that gifts of the Holy Spirit can be used in destroying the kingdom of darkness.

5 KEY POINTS FOR OPERATING IN SPIRITUAL GIFTS

Before we look at an overview of spiritual gifts, it is important for us to explore the points below. There are 5 key points to know for anyone operating in the gifts of the Holy Spirit.

1. Recognise the Source and Purpose

In 1 Corinthians 12:11 it says *'But one and the same Spirit works all these things, distributing to each one individually as He wills.'* This means that the gifts of the Holy Spirit are given and should be used for God's will and not for our own personal ambitions. If God's gifts are used outside of God's purpose the end result will be destruction. We see this in the life of Balaam whose lust for money and wealth swayed him to use his God given ability in a perverse manner, which invited God's judgment to come upon Balaam (Numbers 22). This is also why the apostles rebuked a man's request to buy the power and gifts of God in Acts 8:20. The gifts of God cannot and should not be bought with money or used for any moneymaking business.

In 1 Peter 4:10 it says *'As each one has received a gift, minister it to one another, as good stewards of the manifold grace of God.'* We see from this verse that gifts are not reserved to only pastors or ordained ministers. It says *'each one has received a gift'* and *'minister it to one another'*. All the saints have been given a gift of grace to serve. God's gifts are for God's purposes and NOT for private use or your own agenda!

2. Have the right motives

In 1 Corinthians 14:1 it says *'Pursue love and desire spiritual gifts….'* This tells us that the motive and methods for using spiritual gifts must be founded on love. The structure of chapters 12-14 of 1st Corinthians reveals some interesting points. Chapter 12 lists the spiritual gifts and Chapter 14 explains how the gifts can operate. However, before we read chapter 14, chapter 13 explains the motive of not just spiritual gifts but our new lives in Christ — LOVE. Love is the purest motive that enables spiritual gifts to be used for God's glory and not our own. We see this in the life of the Lord Jesus Himself. In Matthew 14:14 it says *'when Jesus went out He saw a great multitude, and He was moved with compassion for them, and healed their sick.'* This teaches us that the love of God activated the gift of healing. Interestingly, the fruits of the Spirit will activate the gifts of the Spirit. When our motive is love, we will desire the appropriate gift from God to use for that particular moment. Always check your motives. Pursue love.

3. Some gifts are irrevocable

In Romans 11:29 it says *'for the gifts and calling of God are without repentance.'* The focus of this scripture is not man's decision but God's decision. God will not change His mind on some supernatural graces. Although this highlights His love and mercy, it is also a sobering reality to understand that God's gifts do not mean God's approval. This explains what is written in Matthew 7:21 *'Lord, Lord, have*

> *'God's gifts do not mean Gods approval'*

we not prophesied in your name, cast out demons in your name, and done many wonders in your name?' They were not granted entry into God's kingdom because they had gifts without intimacy and obedience to Jesus. Gifts are important, but they are not the proof that you have been reconciled to the Father! Obedience and the fruits of the Holy Spirit are a sign you have communion with God (Galatians 5:21-22).

4. Gifts make room

Proverbs 18:16 says 'A man's gift makes room for him, and brings him before great men.' To 'make room' is to create a platform or space for the grace of God to be revealed through you. Gifts can create a platform to instruct, rebuke, and preach the gospel and any other divinely inspired reason. The story of Joseph teaches us that the gift of God working through one man changed the economic direction of a whole country. Joseph served the gifts God placed within Him and this lead the people of Egypt out of famine. You lead by serving the gifts God gives you. Not only that but through God given gifts, He can expand His dominion through you. Never underestimate God's ability to reach people and expand His kingdom through you!

5. Act with Confidence

Another word for confidence is assurance. When you operate with spiritual gifts by faith, you should be fully assured that God would perform His Word. Again it says in 1 Peter 4:11 'If anyone ministers, let him do it as with the ability which God supplies, that in all things God may be glorified through Jesus Christ'. This verse teaches us that God's ability accompanies His ministry. When you step out and act by faith, you can be assured that God will reward your confidence (Hebrews 10:35). Our role is to obey Him and His is to perform His word.

WHAT ARE THE NINE GIFTS OF THE HOLY SPIRIT?

The nine gifts of the Holy Spirit in 1 Corinthians 12:8-12 have been typically placed into 3 categories; Revelation, Inspiration/Vocal and Power. Though they can be put into categories, each gift can inspire the manifestation of another; for example word of knowledge brings healing or inspires prophecy. Below is an overview of the 9 spiritual gifts.

Revelation

1. Word of Knowledge

'To another the word of knowledge through the same Spirit,' — 1 Corinthians 12:8

The word 'knowledge' is *'gnosis'* in Greek, which means to know or be aware. A word of knowledge is when the Holy Spirit reveals information or brings awareness to you about another person or place. This information does not come from natural sources but directly from the Holy Spirit. An example of this was in John's Gospel when Jesus told the Samaritan women about the previous relationships she had while they stood at the well (John 4: 1-26). This information came from God directly, and the women then spoke to another person about Jesus and said *'He told me all the things that I ever did.'* The whole city came out to Jesus after hearing the women's experience which lead to many people believing in Him as Messiah.

I was invited to speak at a worship conference in Leicester a year ago. After the altar call, I began to pray for the young people that came to the front. The Holy Spirit inspired me to tell a particular woman that she previously attempted to commit suicide and that God loves her and has kept her alive. She began to weep and then fell under God's power after I commanded that spiritual bondage to break. I received a message on social media two days later from her praising God. She said that tried to commit suicide nine times in three years, but Jesus completely delivered her that night, praise God! God reveals to redeem!

2. Word of Wisdom

'for to one is given the word of wisdom through the Spirit' 1 Corinthians 12:8

The gift of wisdom is when the Holy Spirit empowers you to give godly instruction and judgment. It enables you to apply natural or divine information. This ability does

'The wisdom of God is pure and will reflect Christ's nature!'

not come from personal study of the Bible alone but is given by the Holy Spirit. There are two kinds of wisdom; the wisdom of men and the wisdom of God. The wisdom of men is corrupted by sin and does not lead to righteousness. The wisdom of God is pure and will reflect Christ's nature (James 3:13-17). An example of the gift of wisdom is in 1 Kings 3:16-28 when Solomon gave wise judgment in the case of two women in conflict over a living child after the death of another child. Another example of the gift of wisdom at work is when Jesus spoke to the Pharisees concerning the women caught in the act of adultery (John 8:1-12). His judgment was righteous, and He gave God's perspective, which caused the plot of the religious leaders to be brought to nothing. The gift of wisdom, like other spiritual gifts, works together with other spiritual gifts, such as word of knowledge and discerning of spirits.

3. Discerning of spirits

'to another discerning of spirits' -1 Corinthians 12:9

The word 'discernment' comes from the Greek word *'diakrisis'* which means to separate thoroughly and give a judicial judgment. To be discerning of spirits is to judge accurately which spirit is functioning. It is the God given ability to see and distinguish between divine, demonic and fleshly spiritual operations and manifestations. The sad truth is that it is not only the Spirit of God that is at work in the world. We are warned that in the last days people will fall pray to *'deceiving spirits'* and teachings that are inspired by demons (1 Timothy 4:1).

We see an example of the spiritual gift of discerning of spirits in Acts 16:16-18. Paul was ministering in a place when a slave girl possessed with a spirit of divination began to proclaim that God sent him. Though the information was accurate, Paul discerned that the spirit from which it was coming from was ungodly. He cast the spirit out of the girl and she no longer told fortunes!

It is important to know that every Christian can grow in discernment as they hear and obey the word of God (Hebrews 5:14). There is however, a BIG difference between discernment and a critical spirit. Discernment has analytical abilities that are founded on love. This enables the person to have a clear perspective with righteous judgment and response. A critical spirit is usually based on fear, suspicion, and even rejection; projecting views/lies, they have believed about themselves onto others. 'Seeing' with the wrong heart is dangerous. A heart of love gives the perfect perception and judgment on the things you see. It will inspire the right actions to take and outcome to seek. This explains the importance of Paul's prayer in Philippians 1:9 *'And this I pray, that your love may abound still more and more in knowledge and all discernment.'*

Inspiration

4. Different kinds of tongues

'To another different kinds of tongues' — 1 Corinthians 12:10

The word 'tongues' comes from the Greek word 'glōssa' which means a language not naturally acquired. The gift of tongues is a supernatural language. When the Holy Spirit gives you the gift of tongues, you will be enabled to communicate with God beyond the limitations of your earthly language. God is heavenly. Therefore earthly descriptions and expressions can and will limit you in the place of prayer. The gift of tongues enables you to commune with Him on a much deeper level. There are at least three kinds of tongues the Bible speaks of:

1. **Personal Prayer.** The first way the gift of tongues can manifest is in personal prayer to God. 1 Corinthians 14 details some benefits of speaking in tongues in personal prayer. One is that you are enabled to speak in mystery. This means that you are praying to God from a place beyond your human logic and reasoning. Reasoning and logic can be a hindrance, especially when agreeing with God on things that will challenge your natural understanding. The second benefit is that praying in tongues edifies the person praying. In 1 Corinthians 14:4 it says *'he who speaks in a tongue edifies himself.'* The word edify is 'oikodomeō' in Greek, which means to embolden or to build up. The Holy Spirit infuses a tremendous boldness within you while speaking in tongues during prayer. Our spirits become charged with God's love and power. Revelation begins to open up to you as you engage with God's Spirit in this prayer language. Not only that, but the Holy Spirit nourishes and refreshes your spirit. You drink from a fountain of living water! I challenge you to spend time praying in tongues. Pray in your house, pray in your room, pray in the car and pray on the bus. There is a life of God we can access through this amazing gift of the Holy Spirit.

2 **Tongues for a sign.** The second way the gift of tongues can manifest is a natural language that was acquired supernaturally. We see an example of this on the day of Pentecost when the disciples began to speak with other tongues as the Holy Spirit inspired them. Devout men from places such as Syria, Egypt, Asia and Rome who in shock said *'we hear them speaking in our tongues the wonderful works of God'* (Acts 2:11). Although they were praying using the gift of tongues, the devout men that were nearby heard God being glorified in their own different languages! Why? It was sign that God was truly at work. God through Jesus accepted the Gentiles as well as the Jews. Though the gospel was not preached in tongues, it was a sign that God was at work, which opens the door to share the way of salvation (Acts 2: 6-38).

3 **Tongues that edify the church.** The third way gift of tongues can manifest is when God is speaking to you. In 1 Corinthians 14:5 it says *'for he who prophesies is greater than he who speaks with tongues, unless indeed he interprets, that the church may receive edification.'* This means prophecy will edify a greater number of people because the language is understandable. God giving a great encouragement to His people through the gift of tongues is excellent, however, without interpretation few people will be truly edified and encouraged. With this kind of tongue, it is now God speaking to His church through the one praying with the gift of tongues. When God is communicating a message to His church through a person praying in tongues, interpretation is required.

5. Interpretation of tongues

'To another the interpretation of tongues.' —
1 Corinthians 12:10

'Hermēneia' is the Greek word for interpretation, which means to translate. Originating from Hermes who was known as the messenger god in Greek mythology. The gift of interpretation of tongues is when the Holy Spirit gives you the ability to understand and interpret God's message to His church. When the gift of interpretation accompanies the gift of tongues, a greater number of people can be edified. Those who are mature should judge the authenticity and acuracy of the message being brought forth (1 Corinthians 14:5, 13-14).

6. Prophecy

'..To another prophecy....' — *1 Corinthians 12:10.*

The gift of prophecy is when the Holy Spirit gives a person the ability to communicate divine knowledge or messages to others by the inspiration of God. The word prophecy is *'propheteia'* in Greek, which means prediction through scripture or other. The purpose of prophecy is to testify of Christ (Revelation 19:10). 1 Corinthians 14:3 says that *'he who prophesies speaks edification and exhortation and comfort to men.'* This highlights the threefold

> **'The threefold purpose of the gift of prophecy; exhortation and comfort.'**

purpose of the gift of prophecy; edification, exhortation and comfort. The gift of prophecy will only tear down what is of the devil and establish what is of God (Jeremiah 1:10). It brings both the individual and community into harmony with the purpose and plans of God (Jeremiah 23:22, Ephesians 4:11-16).

I received a message from a youth pastor who had been grateful to God for using us to bring a move of the Holy Spirit in her church. She called me testifying that the prophetic word I gave her had been fulfilled. The prophecy was that Jesus would activate her prophetic ministry with great authority and power. Also, that there would be an eruption of the anointing like a volcano that will cause a shift in her and those around her (church, family and community). She was fasting and praying about the prophetic word she received. She had set in her heart to stand on God's Word and see it fulfilled (1 Timothy 1:18). She was asked to speak in her church a few Sundays after. She stepped out by faith and made an altar call for people who had a desire to serve God but was fearful.

However, when she preached the power of God fell in the church and she began to flow in the gifts of the Spirit! The whole church was turned upside down — all the people fell under the power of God. People began to receive new tongues, dance, were set free. Others received a fresh baptism of fire and the church is simply not the same! Glory be to God! God's words carry God's authority. We can't take glory o when He speaks through us. All we do is represent or deliver His Word, which is His authority (Hebrews 1:1-3).

SHOULD PROPHECY BE JUDGED?

*'Beloved, do not believe every spirit, but test the spirits,
whether they are of God; because many false prophets have
gone out into the world.' — 1 John 4:1*

*'Let two or three prophets speak, and let the others judge.' —
1 Corinthians 14:29*

Yes. To judge in this context means to examine or to determine the validity/authenticity of something. However, we are not to judge prophesy from a place of paranoia. Paranoia is rooted from a place of fear. The Lord requires us to judge from a heart of love, which is where true discernment comes from. This will enable us to examine things and compare them in the light of God's heart and His Word (1 Corinthians 2:14-15, Hebrews 5:14, Philippians 1:9). Here are some questions to ask when judging prophecy:

* Was it fulfilled or is it coming to pass? (Deuteronomy 18:21-22)
* Does it line up with Scripture? (Jeremiah 23:18-31).
* Does it bring me closer to the Lord/Glorify God? (John 16:13-14)
* Does it bring liberty or bondage and confusion? (1 Corinthians 14:33)
* Is there an inner witness? (1 John 2:27)

Power

7. Faith

'To another faith by the same Spirit' — 1 Corinthians 12:9

The Greek word for faith is *'pistis'* which means conviction, trust, belief and confidence. Although every saint has the measure of faith to rely on Christ for salvation (Ephesians 2:8-9, Romans 12:4), the Holy Spirit gives the gift of faith to enable for unshakable confidence in the promises of God. Hebrews 11 details people who have walked in the gift of faith, which enabled them to make a great stand and impact in their generation.

8. Healing

*'To another gifts of healings by the same Spirit,' —
1 Corinthians 12:9*

The gift of healing is when the Holy Spirit cures all kinds of sickness and diseases through the prayers of the saints. God revealed Himself to Israel in the Old Testament as Jehovah Rapha, which means 'The God who heals.' Jesus continued revealing this in His earthly ministry as a sign of God's Kingdom. God still works through this gift to continue to reveal the promise He to all who trust in Jesus. Healing is an act of war against the kingdom of darkness. Anything that is not in Heaven we can pray for to be healed. In Acts 3:1-10 we read an account of Peter healing a man who was lame. What is amazing is that contemporaries would have frowned upon Peter's method of delivery today, as it breaks religious mindsets and some charismatic theology. Peter did not speak to God about the sickness, he spoke to the man and gave a word of command *'in the name of Jesus Christ of Nazareth, get up and walk.'* He then took the man and lifted him and his ankles received strength. Also, the Bible says that Jesus was moved with compassion and healed the multitude. The fruits of the Spirit will activate the gifts of the Spirit.

During my lunch break I met a man called John at the chips shop over the road from where I was doing a social work placement. John was on crutches for years after falling and shattering his hip over 12 years ago. After asking him about it he said the pain was excruciating. I put my hand on his side and spoke healing to his body in Jesus' name. The power of God touched him and he was healed! He confirmed that there was no pain and walked without crutches to get his fish and chips for the first time in years.

I was also invited to speak at an event in Luton. After speaking on Matthew 8:1-4 a woman came to receive healing in her jaw that had been locked and caused her pain for years. As she received prayer, I could feel her jaw clicking and loosening as God's power was touching her. However, in spite of this she was not fully restored. I could not help but wonder why this was. However, in spite of feeling slightly discouraged, I gave God thanks for completing the healing after the event when she returned home.

A couple of days later I received an amazing message that she was completely healed! Her mouth was loosened and she now has complete movement in her jaw! Praise God! Jesus heals! It is our hands but His power! What this particular event taught me was that my respon-

'Anything that is not in Heaven we can pray to be healed.'

sibility is to obey Him, rather than consider the fear of failure. I would encourage you to take a risk and see God's healing power work in people.

9. Miracles

'To another the working of miracles,' — *1 Corinthians 12:10*

The word miracle is 'dunamis' in Greek, which means miracle working power, force or violence. The gift of working miracles is when the Holy Spirit works through you, to bring about an event of supernatural power. This manifestation of power demonstrates the authority of Jesus Christ and sovereignty of God's Kingdom. Miracles defy the laws of nature and simply can only be explained as an act of God to make Himself known. Biblical miracles always were for the purpose of directing people to God. Jesus performed many miracles in the Gospel. One notable miracle was when He raised Lazarus from the dead (John 11).

In 2 Corinthians 12:12 Paul said *'Truly the signs of an apostle were accomplished among you with all perseverance, in signs and wonders and mighty deeds.'* Miracles, signs and wonders were also a sign of the ministry of the apostles. This can be from raising the dead, healings and deliverance (Acts 9:36-42, Acts 19:11-12).

In Mark 16:17 it says *'...these signs will follow those who believe: In My name, they will cast out demons; they will speak with new tongues....'* This means miracles are not exclusive to apostles. Miracles, signs and wonders do not follow positions, experience or titles but faith.

CAN SPIRITUAL GIFTS BECOME INACTIVE?

'Therefore I remind you to stir up the gift of God which is in you through the laying on of my hands. For God has not given us a spirit of fear, but of power and of love and of a sound mind.' — *2 Timothy 1:6-7*

It is possible that after receiving spiritual gifts that they can become dormant or inactive in the life of a Christian. The Bible highlights one major reason — fear. Fear in the above context means 'cowardice.' In other words, fear makes you a coward. Fear can cause life and freedom to be restricted and gifts to be made dormant. Fear brings a person into bondage (Romans 8:15). It restricts them from expressing their God given gifts. It renders people to be inactive and can quench the Spirit of God from working freely in their lives. Fear makes you self conscious instead of God conscious. We see this in the book of Kings when Elijah ran from Jezebel even after a great victory had been won against the prophets of Baal (1 Kings 18-19).

3 WAYS TO OVERCOME FEAR AND KEEP SPIRITUAL GIFTS ACTIVE

Before reading any further, it is vital for you to understand that Jesus Christ makes men fearless. We know this because the attributes of Gods intended nature for man are highlighted —love, power and a sound mind. 'FEAR NOT' is written 365 times in the Bible; once for every day of the year. God knew that this spirit could hinder Him from freely working through us. It is simply not God's plan for us to be afraid. Imagine what your life would be like without fear? Listed below are three ways in which the Bible teaches us to overcome fear and keep spiritual gifts stirred within us.

Love — The first way we can overcome fear is by walking in love (1 John 4:8). A lot of times people talk about biblical love in a flaky or sensual way, but the Bible shows that our love for God is expressed in our obedience to Him (1 John 2:3-5). Christ conquered sin and overcame all obstacles in the world; He obeyed God completely (John 16:33). We are more than conquerers through faith in Him (1 John 4:4) and are given the power to obey (love) Him and know Him. Obedience through faith in Christ is our authority over fear.

Fear of God — The second way to combat fear is to fear the right thing (Proverbs 14:26). The Bible says the fear of the Lord produces confidence. When we fear God, there is nothing else to fear. What is the difference between the fear of God and being afraid of God? Being afraid of God makes you run from Him because of sin and misunderstanding of The Cross. People who are afraid of God are afraid to be near Him (Genesis 3:8-10, Exodus 20:18-19). The fear of God is that you are afraid to be away from Him, and therefore run towards Him (Exodus 20:20). Those who fear Him see His greatness. Knowledge of His judgment seat will deliver you from being intimidated by people because you are living in view of eternity (2 Corinthians 5:9-11, Matthew 10:27-31). In other words, you serve who you fear. God does not just want us to respect Him but to have a loving relationship with Him through Jesus. The fear of God will deliver you from the fear of man.

Prayer — The third way we can combat fear is through continually praying. In 2 Timothy 1:6-7 it says —'*Therefore I remind you to stir up the gift of God, which is in you through the laying on of my hands.*' The word 'stir' in Greek is 'anazōpureō', which means to rekindle or fan into flames. The disciples saw Jesus ascend into Heaven but still needed to pray for boldness, how much more us! (Acts 4:29-30). They continued in prayer, fellowship, communion and the apostles teaching. The Holy Spirit was then able to work freely through them. If you continue in these things, you will keep God's gifts within you active and maintain victory over fear.

CONCLUSION

Pursue love, and desire spiritual gifts, but especially that you may prophesy." — *1 Corinthians 14:1*

We should desire to reach and serve people using spiritual gifts. Whether you have just started a relationship with Jesus or have been walking with Him for a long period, make no mistake about it; God can use you. Christ not only transferred His identity to us, He also transferred His ministry. Do you need to stir up the gifts with you? Maybe fear has held you from operating in spiritual gifts or a past mistake. Regardless of the reason, God's love liberates and I command the bondage of fear to break off your life in Jesus' name! A minister once said '*God can use a failure but He cannot use a quitter*'. Stir up the gift in you by confronting the spirit of fear and experience the love and peace of God in your heart. If you have not trusted in Jesus please know that the greatest gifts God has given us are forgiveness and salvation (Ephesians 2:8-9). Turn from sin and put your trust in Jesus and you will become a child of God.

CHAPTER 6 — GIFTS OF THE HOLY SPIRIT: PERSONAL STUDY

1. Memories 1 Corinthians 13:13 and 1 Corinthians 14:1

2. According 1 Corinthians 13, why is love essential? How does love relate to desiring the best gift?

   _____

   _____

   _____

3. Write your own definition of the nine gifts of the Holy Spirit mentioned in 1 Corinthians 12:7-11

   _____

   _____

   _____

   _____

4. According to the following scriptures, how can you stir up the gift of God within you? How can you overcome fear? 2 Timothy 1:6-7, Acts 4:29-30, Proverbs 14:26, 1 John 4:18

   _____

   _____

   _____

   _____

5. CHALLENGE. Step out and pray for someone today, and share the gospel. Ask God for the best gift as you act by faith and love. Write your reflections below.

   _____

   _____

   _____

   _____

CHAPTER 7: RESURRECTION

'Jesus said to her, 'I am the resurrection and the life. He who believes in me, though he may die, he shall live.' — John 11:25

INTRODUCTION

The strap line for this present generation is 'YOLO' — 'You only live once'. This is one of the biggest lies of the adversary because there is a life after this one. How we live in this life has a direct impact on our experience of eternity in the afterlife. What does the Bible say about resurrection and the afterlife? Why is Jesus' resurrection so significant? How does this impact on our daily lives? As we seek to explore these questions, may God's Spirit revive and renew you. May it inspire you to make your day's count and make you sober to live in view of eternity, in Jesus' name. Amen.

WHAT IS RESURRECTION?

Resurrection comes from the Greek word *'anastasis'* which means a standing up again, raised to life again, or rising again. The Bible teaches that death is not the end of human existence. Resurrection is the event by which those who died will rise again to live in the afterlife. Resurrection can also mean the moral recovery of spiritual truth. See the scripture below:

'Then you shall know that I am the Lord, when I have opened your graves, O My people, and brought you up from your graves. I will put My Spirit in you, and you shall live, and I will place you in your land. Then you shall know that I, the Lord, have spoken it and performed it,' says the Lord.' — Ezekiel 37:12-14

'Resurrection is the event by which those who died will rise again to the afterlife.'

'Then you shall know that I AM the Lord.' God gives us three signs that reveal He is the Lord; resurrection, life and inheritance. He declares 'when I have opened your graves, O My people, and brought you up from your graves' which teaches us that His power to resurrect is key in recognising and submitting to His lordship. It also demonstrates His dominion over the grave and the power over death. He goes on to say 'I will put My Spirit in you, and you shall live' to help us understand that our lives are only sustained by His Holy Spirit and in Him alone, we can now live. Finally, God declares 'I will place you in your own land' which teaches us that through Him we have received a place of possession or land of inheritance. Interestingly, Jesus declares in John 11:25 'I am the resurrection and the life. He who believes in me, though he may die, he shall live.'

During Ezekiel's time, the house of Israel was scattered and barren. God declared that they would know Him as the Lord by His ability to resurrect them from the grave, gather them together and fill them with His Spirit. Resurrection is a sign of God's authority over death.

WHAT DOES THE BIBLE SAY ABOUT THE AFTERLIFE?

> 'Do not marvel at this; for the hour is coming in which all who are in the graves will hear His voice and come forth—those who have done good, to the resurrection of life, and those who have done evil, to the resurrection of condemnation.' — John 5:38

> 'For the Lord He will descend from heaven with a shout, with the voice of an archangel, and with the trumpet of God. And the dead in Christ will rise first.' — 1 Thessalonians 4:16

God's word encourages saints to recognise the realities that follow the afterlife. In fact Paul wrote 'But I do not want you to be ignorant, brethren, concerning those who have fallen asleep, lest you sorrow as others who have no hope.' Paul admonished the saints in Thessalonica not to be ignorant about the afterlife and imparted hope to their lives. The word 'afterlife' is 'Olam Haba' in Hebrew, which means age or the world to come. The afterlife is the place and state where a person will live in eternally after they die. The Bible teaches us that there are at least two resurrections for the afterlife; the resurrection to life and the resurrection of condemnation.

FIRST RESURRECTION

'And I saw thrones, and they sat on them, and judgment was committed to them. Then I saw the souls of those who had been beheaded for their witness to Jesus and for the word of God, who had not worshiped the beast or his image, and had not received his mark on their foreheads or on their hands. And they lived and reigned with Christ for a thousand years. But the rest of the dead did not live again until the thousand years were finished. This is the first resurrection. Blessed and holy is he who has part in the first resurrection. Over such the second death has no power, but they shall be priests of God and of Christ, and shall reign with Him a thousand years.' — Revelations 20:4-6*

The first resurrection is of life. Those that will be at this resurrection are people who have put their trust in Christ for salvation. In 1 Thessalonians 4:16 it says *'The dead in Christ will rise first.'* God has never judged the righteous with the wicked. At Christ's 2nd coming, He defeats the beast, false

> *'They will be made kings and priests to God and serve Him forever.'*

prophet and then binds Satan with chains in the bottomless pit for a thousand years. Jesus will then establish His government on Earth. Those who died in Christ will be raised first and appear at His Judgment seat and they will be rewarded for their life of faith in Christ (see chapter 8). Thrones and authority will be committed to them to judge on behalf of God. They will be made kings and priests to God and serve Him forever (1 Corinthians 15:23-24). Death will no longer have any power over them!

There are three key characteristics of those that God will grant the first resurrection (see Revelation 20:4-6).

Witnesses of Jesus — They publically and privately testified to the resurrection of Jesus Christ. These people proclaimed the gospel of Jesus with their lives even to the point of death. In 2 Timothy 3:12 it says *'Yes, and all who desire to live godly in Christ Jesus will suffer persecution.'* Persecution does not destroy you, it purifies your faith and enables you to commune with God and cultivates Christ like character.

Did not worship the beast — In Matthew 24:4 Jesus warns us to '...*Take heed that no man deceive you.*' Deception is the way Satan leads people away from God and into destruction. People will be deceived into submitting to the beast's authority by worshipping its image. We see a picture of this in the book of Daniel when King Nebuchadnezzar commanded his subjects to worship the image he created as a symbol of submission to his authority (Daniel 3:7). However, at the first resurrection God will raise those '*who had not worshipped the beast or his image*'. These are believers who have studied to show themselves approved to God and refuse to submit to the false teachings and lies; regardless of the opposition. With the level of deception and false teachers out there, you cannot afford to neglect personal study of the Word of God. False teachers and prophets exploit the biblical illiteracy of people (Isaiah 5:13). Do not allow someone to take advantage of your ignorance. Study to show yourself approved to God! (2Timothy 2:15). If it is not in line or context with ALL scripture, Christ's character and The Gospel then do not buy into it! Period.

Did not receive his mark — Rulers of kingdoms would have their image engraved on coins, gold and other materials as a symbol of their rulership and authority. We see this throughout history and in the time when Christ first came (Matthew 20:20-21). However, the objects being marked are no longer coins but people. The 'foreheads' or their 'hands' are the areas that the beast would engrave as a symbol of its authority over them. Though there may be a physical meaning, there is also a figurative meaning. The hands can symbolize our works, where as our head can refer to our mind. This can mean the mark of the beast is to be sealed by the flesh in your mind and works. The Saints that did not worship the beast or receive its image will be granted the first resurrection.

WHAT IS THE PURPOSE OF HEAVEN?

'God didn't make man for rulership of Heaven, He made him for the rulership of Earth.'

Heaven is God's first estate. It is Gods throne and centre of His Government. Another name the Bible uses to describe this place is 'glory' (Col 3:4). A place of unspeakable pleasure and glory reserved for God and His children. It's important to understand that God didn't make man for the rulership of Heaven; He made him for the rulership of Earth. In Psalm 115:16 it says *'The heaven, even the heavens, are the Lord's; But the earth He has given to the children of men.'* Heaven is the domain in which God rules from, but earth is the domain God has given man to rule. The Gospel is not only about God reconciling man back to Himself; it is also about restoring Earth back under man's authority. After death, God's people will go to Heaven and be in glory with Jesus. However, for His eternal purpose for humankind to be fulfilled, He must return man to a new Earth (Isaiah 65:17, 2 Peter 3:1, Revelation 21:1). In the age to come, the new Earth will not be corrupted by sin and death. Man will be able to fulfill the dominion that Adam lost in the Garden of Eden. In the age to come those who rise again at Christ's coming will reign with Him. They will see God's perfect will be done 'on earth as it is in Heaven.'

SECOND RESURRECTION

'Then I saw a great white throne and Him who sat on it, from whose face the earth and the heaven fled away. And there was found no place for them. And I saw the dead, small and great, standing before God, and books were opened. And another book was opened, which is the Book of Life. And the dead were judged according to their works, by the things which were written in the books. The sea gave up the dead who were in it, and Death and Hades delivered up the dead who were in them. And they were judged, each one according to his works. Then Death and Hades were cast into the lake of fire. This is the second death. And anyone not found written in the Book of Life was cast into the lake of fire.' - Revelations 20:11-15

There is no greater tragedy than to deny Jesus. The second resurrection is for those who have refused to accept God's salvation through Jesus. After the

> *'There is no greater tragedy than to deny Jesus.'*

thousand year period, all those who died in sin will stand before The Great White Throne of Judgment and then be cast into the lake of fire. Even death and hell will be cast there along with the devil. This judgement is the victory of the final enemy — death. Tragically, although hell was created for the devil, many will deny God's gift and choose this place. Even many Christians have neglected the reality of this place and professed to know God but denied Him by their actions. God does not desire for anyone to perish but for all to repent of their sin and believe in Jesus. This is called the second death.

IS THERE A PURPOSE FOR HELL?

Hell is very real and there is a purpose for it. Hell or *'Sheol'* in Hebrew means 'the underworld' 'grave' 'pit' or 'prison.' It is the destination for those who have refused to repent of sin and trust in Jesus for salvation. It is a place of eternal punishment and is absent of all the attributes of God (love, peace, hope, joy, light). In Matthew 25:41 it says 'Then He will also say to those on the left hand, 'Depart from Me, you cursed, into the everlasting fire prepared for the devil and his angels.' This teaches us that hell was prepared for the devil and his angels but NOT for humankind. Tragically, through deception people choose to follow in Satan's rebellion toward God. Because of following Satan, they receive the same penalty for rebellion. Humanity was created by God and for God (Colossians 1:16). Man is the object of God's love.

IS RESURECTION A FUTURE EVENT ONLY?

No. The resurrection is not only an event at the end of the age. The resurrection is a person — Jesus Christ. He is the *'God who gives life to the dead and calls those things that are not as though they are'*. In addition, He not only has the authority to raise the dead but He keeps and sustains them by His power. Romans 8:11 says the *'if Spirit of Him who raised Jesus from the dead dwells in you, He who raised Christ from the dead will also give life to your mortal bodies through His Spirit who dwells in you.'* We have the same Spirit that raised Christ from the dead living in us. Jesus cannot be in a place and anything remains the same. See the scripture below:

> *'The Resurrection is not only an event at the end of the age. The resurrection is a person — Jesus Christ.'*

*'Jesus said to her, 'I am the resurrection and the life. He who
believes in me, though he may die, he shall live.' — John 11:25*

The tradition that was held was that after four days a body could never rise
from the dead. What they understand was that resurrection was only a
future event and not a present reality (John 11:24). However, when Jesus
came onto the scene the whole situation broke their tradition and
'theology'. He is the resurrection! In Christ, anything that was dead can be
raised to life. He can change any minus into plus in an instant. Regardless of
social status, history, crime or time. He is the resurrection and He lives
inside us by the Holy Spirit, praise God! He is within us, which gives us the
power to raise anything around us to life in Jesus' name!

WHAT IS THE SIGNIFICANCE OF CHRIST'S RESURRECTION?

Christ Jesus did not only raise others from the dead; He also rose again
from the dead Himself. The resurrection is central to Christian faith. Why?
What is the significance? Listed below are several reasons why Christ
resurrection is significant:

PROVED HE IS THE SON OF GOD

Romans 1:4 says *'concerning His Son Jesus Christ our Lord, who was born of
the seed of David according to the flesh, and declared to be the Son of God
with power according to the Spirit of holiness, by the resurrection from the
dead.'*. When religious leaders challenged Jesus' authority, He would
constantly refer to His
Father. He even declared
that He and His Father are
one, which offended them
and made them seek to kill
Him (John 10:30-32).

**'His Resurrection declared His
Sonship.'**

However, when Christ rose again it confirmed that God was His Father and
all that He did was in the Father's name (John 10:17-19). His Resurrection
declared His Sonship.

PROVED JESUS HAS POWER OVER DEATH AND HELL

Romans 6:9 says *'knowing that Christ, having been raised from the dead, dies no more. Death no longer has dominion over Him.'* Death was the enemy that prevented the priests from offering sacrifices to God to make atonement for themselves and the people (Hebrews 8:23). Death bound every man since the fall of Adam and no one had the power to overcome death's reign in the Earth. However, Christ demonstrated His power over death by being raised from the dead praise God! Anyone who trusts in Him will be granted

'Anyone who trusts in Him will be granted resurrection in Him.'

resurrection in His likeness. Through Christ we can boldly declare what is written in 1 Corinthians 15:55, *'O Death, where is your sting? O Hades, where is your victory?'*

PROVED THAT JESUS' BLOOD MAKES ATONEMENT FOR SIN FOREVER

'For the life of the flesh is in the blood, and I have given it to you upon the altar to make atonement for your souls; for it is the blood that makes atonement for the soul.' — Leviticus 17:11

As we mentioned in Chapter 1, atonement is when God covers man's sin to restore him to fellowship with God without the consequence of death. In the Old Testament, only temporary atonement could be made through the blood of bulls and rams. See the scripture below:

'For if the blood of bulls and goats and the ashes of a heifer, sprinkling the unclean, sanctifies for the purifying of the flesh, how much more shall the blood of Christ, who through the eternal Spirit offered Himself without spot to God, cleanse your conscience from dead works to serve the living God?' — Hebrews 9:13-14

Christ's resurrection proved that God accepted His blood to cover sin eternally. Within the blood of Jesus is eternal life and the power of resurrection praise God! His resurrection proved that Jesus' blood has the power to cleanse us from sin. Those who trust in Him will be cleansed by His blood and raised to life with Him. Blood is not literal but spiritual and releases the power of resurrection life to those who believe.

PROVED JESUS IS SURETY OF THE NEW COVENANT

Hebrews 7:22 says 'by so much more Jesus has become a surety of a better covenant.' Surety means a pledge given in a covenant between two people. At the last supper, Jesus declared that His body and blood were the foundations of the new covenant between God and man. His resurrection declared that God accepted Jesus' sacrifice on The Cross. We can now understand what Paul said in Romans 8:32: 'He who did not spare His own Son, but delivered Him up for us all, how shall He not with Him also freely give us all things? 'Jesus' Resurrection declared that we have eternal security with the Father through faith in the Son.

EXAMPLE OF A GLORIED BODY

After Jesus' resurrection, we read accounts in the Gospel of Him eating, drinking and moving from location to location. He ate food but was sustained by His Father. This gives us an understanding of how our glorified bodies will function. Eating and drinking may have originally only been for pleasure. We were created to live by *'every word that proceeds from the mouth of God'* (Due 8:3).

CONCLUSION

Beloved, now we are children of God; and it has not yet been revealed what we shall be, but we know that when He is revealed, we shall be like Him, for we shall see Him as He is. And everyone who has this hope in Him purifies himself, just as He is pure.' — 1 John 3:2-3

Which resurrection will you be present at? God does not want anyone to perish or be found at the second resurrection; He is willing for all to repent and be saved through Jesus. The resurrection is not just an event at the end of the age; the resurrection is a Person - Jesus Christ. God has confirmed that we can trust Jesus by raising Him from the dead. He is our Living Hope who has power over death and Satan. God can resurrect anything; dead relationships, finances and most importantly your soul. A minister once said *'the Gospel is not about bad people turning good, it is about dead people being brought to life.'* In Christ Jesus, we receive eternal life. Trust in Him and see resurrection in your life and those around you.

CHAPTER 7 — RESURRECTION: PERSONAL STUDY

1. Scripture to remember is John 11:25

2. Using the following scriptures, summarise the 1st and 2nd Resurrection in your own words. 1 Thessalonians 4:16, Revelation 20:1-6 and Revelation 20:11-15

    _____

    _____

    _____

    _____

3. According to the following scriptures, is resurrection an event in the future only? If not, think of practical examples of how we can experience and apply the power of resurrection today? John 11:25, Romans 8:11, Acts 1:4-8

    _____

    _____

    _____

    _____

4. According to the following scriptures, why was Jesus' resurrection significant? Romans 1:1-4, Romans 6:9, 2 Corinthians 4:14, Hebrews 9:13-14, Leviticus 17:11

    _____

    _____

    _____

    _____

5. Reflect on areas in your life that need the power of resurrection (relationships, family, finance, health, relationship with Jesus etc.). Pray for God's resurrection power to touch those areas of your life now.

CHAPTER 8: ETERNAL JUDGMENTS

'Therefore we make it our aim, whether present or absent, to be well pleasing to Him. For we must all appear before the judgment seat of Christ' — 2 Corinthians 5:9-11

INTRODUCTION

It is interesting that some people say 'heavenly minded and no earthly good,'. However, when we truly have a heavenly mindset we will be ignited to number our days and make every day count on earth! The idea of eternity can be difficult for human beings to comprehend, but this does not remove its reality. Truly if we gained a glimpse of eternity, we would be delivered from complacency and seek God's purpose and perspective of success - not our own. What are eternal Judgements? What are the benefits of an eternal perspective? Will there be eternal rewards? If so, what are they? This chapter will answer such questions as we explore what the Word of God says about eternal judgements. I pray that holy fear would be imparted within you and passion to pursue God's purpose for your life. As you read, may you be driven by eternity in Jesus' name? Amen.

WHAT DOES JUDGEMENT SEAT MEAN?

Judgment means a decision after an investigation. The Hebrew word for 'seat' is *'bema'*, which means a raised platform, judicial seat, judgment seat or throne. There were various earthly examples of a judgement seat in the Bible.

Pontus Pilate sat on the judgment seat when he commanded Jesus to be crucified because of the envy of the Jewish leaders (John 19:13). The Jews brought Paul before the judgement seat during the time when Gallio was governor of Achaia. Herod sat on his throne/judgment seat when addressing the people of Tyre and Sidon (Acts 12:20-24, Acts 18:12-17). The bema was the throne of the one who was in authority. It was a seat of power in which the one in charge could judge, command or reward.

The earthly judgement seats were a reflection of the Throne in Heaven. However, the judgements, commands and rewards of earthly kings were limited to time, but God, the King of Kings gives commands, rewards and judgements that last forever! God's authority is absolute and the divine decisions made at His judgement seat are eternal. Have a look at the scriptures below:

> *'I know that whatever God does, it shall be forever. Nothing can be added to it, and nothing taken from it. God does it, that men should fear before Him.'* — *Ecclesiastes 3:11*

> *'Now to the King eternal, immortal, invisible, to God who alone is wise, be honour and glory forever and ever. Amen.'* — *1 Timothy 1:17*

FIVE BENEFITS OF HAVING AN ETERNAL PERSPECTIVE

The definition of eternal is 'lasting for all time without beginning or end'. To better comprehend this we must look to the source of eternity — God. God is eternal, and therefore all that He says and does will be eternal (Ecclesiastes 3:11). An eternal perspective simply means that you are aware of God, eternal judgements and live in view of eternity. There are many benefits of having an eternal perspective, five of which are listed below:

1. Endurance

2 Timothy 2:12 says 'If we endure, we shall also reign with Him.' This verse indicates that a person's capacity to endure with Jesus on Earth will determine the extent that they reign with Him in the afterlife. When we attach an eternal purpose to present challenges, we will have a greater ability to endure hardships. Actually, we would be able to rejoice in hardship and endure things that others cannot endure because we recognise that God will reward us. An eternal perspective will impart divine hope in God, which anchors our souls while going through challenges. This enables us to endure beyond our ability. Romans 8:18 says *'For I consider that the sufferings of this present time are not worthy to be compared with the glory which shall be revealed in us.'* An eternal perspective affects greater strength to endure hardship.

2. Time Management

God calls us to live our lives by assignment and not by accident. An eternal perspective will spark a passion for making the most out of your time on Earth! In Psalm 90 Moses offers up prayer describing the eternal nature of God and man's frailty. After declaring *'Even from everlasting to everlasting, you are God.'* Moses then goes on to say *'So teach us to number our days that we may gain a heart of wisdom'* (Psalm 90:12). After Moses had a glimpse of eternity, he became conscious of his mortality! When we have an eternal perspective, we start to examine our time and seek

> *'An Eternal perspective will provoke you to live life by assignment and not by accident'*

God's wisdom on how to best use it for His glory. Have you numbered your days? If a man were to live for seventy years, it would be equal to 25,550 days on Earth. God has said that our days are written in His book (Psalm 139:16). This does not merely mean count your days but recognise they will end. With that in mind, time will be more precious and we will be far less likely to take our time for granted. An eternal perspective makes you very careful of that word 'later'. This word can destroy relationships, make you procrastinate on goals and leave things undone. It will impart urgency in your heart and make you want to do things today before 'later' becomes 'to late'. An eternal perspective will provoke you to live your life by assignment and not by accident.

3. The Fear of God

2 Corinthians 5:9-11 says *'Knowing, therefore, the terror of the Lord we persuade men....'* What was this terror or fear that Apostle Paul was referring to? It was the judgement seat of Christ. The knowledge of the eternal judgment inspired the fear of God that provoked him to preach the Gospel to others in a fearless and sober way. When we fear God, there is nothing else to fear. Being afraid of God means you are afraid to be near Him because of sin, but the holy fear of God will cause you to want to be near Him. It is a holy reverence that we receive when we recognise God's place of authority and sovereignty. All power originates from God's throne. This knowledge will provoke you to seek

> *'When we fear God there is nothing else to fear'*

God's wisdom (Proverbs 1:7). This wisdom is not given to the intellectual alone but is found in the Person of Jesus. What it inspires is to consecrate ourselves to God because He has given us an eternal promise (1 John 3:3).

4. Private Accountability

Knowledge of the judgement seat will cause you to live as if you will give an account to God for both your public and private life. Hebrews 4:13 says *'And there is no creature hidden from His sight, but all things are naked and open to the eyes of Him to whom we must give account.'* With this knowledge, we seek to live before the audience of only One. It is better to be unpopular with men and popular with God, than be popular with men but God does not know you. When we recognise that we will give an account to God, we seek to live integral and more accountable to Him for our decisions and actions.

5. Discipline and Stewardship

> *'His lord said to him, 'Well done, good and faithful servant; you have been faithful over a few things, I will make you ruler over many things. Enter into the joy of your lord.' — Matthew 25:23*

An eternal perspective will inspire you to be faithful with your abilities and the responsibilities God has given you. The parable of the talents teaches us that God will reward those that are faithful with their responsibilities. The issue of reward was not based upon the amount of abilities but faithfulness. Heaven in this parable is described as 'the joy of the Lord'. This is the same 'joy' that was set before Jesus and gave Him the ability to endure The Cross.

When you are aware that God will judge how you have managed the things He entrusted to you, it will provoke you to be disciplined and faithful. Discipline is not as painful as regret. Regret was the end result for the last servant that buried the talent that was given to him until the day the king judged him. An eternal perspective will provoke you to be a faithful and disciplined steward of the responsibilities God has entrusted you with on Earth.

WHAT WILL JUDGEMENT BE BASED ON?

> *'And if anyone hears my words and does not believe, I do not judge him; for I did not come to judge the world but to save*

the world. He who rejects me, and does not receive my words, has that which judges him—the word that I have spoken will judge him in the last day." John 12:47-48.

This teaches us that on the 'last day' all men will be judged based upon the word of God spoken through Jesus Christ. There will be no surprises for the basis of Gods eternal judgments on that Day. Why? Because God has already given us His word and this will be the basis of His judgement.

WHO WILL BE OUR JUDGE?

'For the Father judges no one, but has committed all judgement to the Son, that all should honour the Son just as they honour the Father.' — John 5:22

Jesus is the Saviour of our sins but will also be our Judge. The Bible says, God the Father has granted His Son Jesus authority to Judge on His behalf. After all things are put under His authority, Jesus will give all things to the Father. Christ's mission to rescue us from sin reveals Him as a saviour but Him receiving authority to judge on behalf of the Father shows Him to be Lord. Romans 2:16 says *'in the day when God will judge the secrets of men by Jesus Christ, according to my gospel.'* God made every man, therefore every man must give an account to God for how they have lived their lives (Hebrews 4:13).

Matthew 12:36 says *'But I say to you that for every idle word men may speak, they will give account of it in the Day of Judgement.'* This means that our words, motives and actions will be examined before God on the Day of Judgement.

WHAT IS THE PURPOSE OF THE JUDGEMENT SEAT OF CHRIST?

The purpose of the judgement seat of Christ is to examine the life that the saint has lived after faith in Jesus. It is not a place of condemnation, as they have trusted in Jesus for salvation. However, eternal rewards will be given based on how believers lived and served God while being on Earth. This will range from receiving a full reward to receiving no reward. Have a look at the scripture below:

'Each one's work will become clear; for the Day will declare it, because it will be revealed by fire; and the fire will test each one's work, of what sort it is. If anyone's work, which he has built on, it, endures, he will receive a reward. If anyone's work is burned, he will suffer loss; but he himself will be saved, yet so as through fire.' — 1 Corinthians 3:13-15

The judgement seat of Christ is the platform by which God judges our actions, motives and words. They will be tried through fire and only that which is pure in the sight of God will remain and be rewarded. The love of God does not increase based on your performance, neither does it decrease based upon your failure. BUT your experience and eternity is affected by your response to the Gospel of Jesus.

ETERNAL REWARDS

The Bible highlights various rewards that will be given at the Judgement Seat of Christ throughout the Bible. We will now look at the heavenly crowns that the Bible says will be rewarded to the saints.

An Incorruptible Crown

'And everyone who competes for the prize is temperate in all things. Now they do it to obtain a perishable crown, but we for an imperishable crown.' — 1 Corinthians 9:25

God will reward The Incorruptible or Imperishable Crown to saints for their perseverance, self-discipline and temperance. Paul describes the Christian walk as a race that has rules or guidelines that must be followed to be eligible to 'compete.' Athletes are required to deny themselves from certain activities or even foods to compete and win. This is also the same for saints to live a life of faith in Christ. Hebrews 12:2 also says that in order to run this race, we must lay aside any besetting sin or weight. Those that deny themselves and persevere will receive an imperishable crown from God.

The Crown of Life

'Blessed is the man who endures temptation; for when he has been approved, he will receive the crown of life which the Lord has promised to those who love Him.' — James 1:12

God will reward The Crown of Life or the Martyr's Crown to saints for patiently enduring temptation, trial and for being faithful to Christ unto death. Christ also promised this crown to the saints in Smyrna that remained faithful to God in the midst of persecution (Revelations 2:10). Those who *'love Him'* are those who kept God's commandments (1 John 2:8, John 14:15). Paul gave a profound encouragement in 2 Corinthians 4, alluding to the saints that the trying of his flesh was revealing the power of Christ in and through his body. Oh if we could grasp this revelation! This also means that you will receive supernatural life from God after enduring hardship. The saints that obey God regardless of trials or persecution will receive the crown of life.

The Crown of Rejoicing

For what is our hope, or joy, or crown of rejoicing? Is it not even you in the presence of our Lord Jesus Christ at His coming?' — 1 Thessalonians 2:19

God will reward the Crown of Rejoicing or 'Soul Winners Crown' to the saints that have been effective witnesses to the lost on Earth. How do we know this? In Philippians 4:1 Paul writes *'therefore, my beloved and longed-for brethren, my joy and crown, so stand fast in the Lord, beloved.'* He describes the people that he converted to Christ through the Gospel as crowns. Although people are not our reward, God will reward in the form of a crown the saints that bring others to salvation. There are three characteristics of this crown — hope, joy and rejoicing. It is very possible that these are the characteristics that these saints imparted into the lives of others on earth also.

The Crown of Righteousness

'Finally, there is laid up for me the crown of righteousness, which the Lord, the righteous Judge, will give to me on that Day, and not to me only but also to all who have loved His appearing.' — 2 Timothy 4:8

'The Lord rewarded me according to my righteousness; According to the cleanness of my hands He has recompensed me." Psalm 20:20

God will reward the saints The Crown of Righteousness for living in the light of Christ's return and loving His appearing. What does it mean to love the Lords appearing? There are particular characteristics of those who live their Christian life in light and anticipation of Christ's return.

Purity and Sanctification — In 1 John 3:3 it says *'everyone who has this hope in Him purifies himself, just as He is pure.'* This means that hope in Christ and His return will inspire the saints to sanctify themselves.

Kingdom minded— In Colossians 3:1-two it says *'If then you were raised with Christ, seek those things which are above, where Christ is, sitting at the right hand of God. Set your mind on things above, not on things on the earth.'* When we know we have been seated with Christ our 'mind set' will be heavenly. The saints that hope in Christ's return will separate their mind from earthly thinking and reasoning. They will live and function in the world but have an earnest desire to cleave to God in word, deed and thought. Their actions will be in light of Gods kingdom and Christ's return.

Spiritual Hunger & Prayer — In Revelation 22:17 it says *'the Spirit and the bride say, 'Come!'* What bride wouldn't want to see her bridegroom? The saints that truly desire His return will have a spiritual hunger that is reflected in prayer and a pursuit of God's purpose for their lives.

The Crown of Glory

> *'And when the Chief Shepherd appears, you will receive the crown of glory that does not fade away.'* — 1 Peter 5:4

God will reward the saints the Crown of Glory for their service to Him as leaders, shepherds, overseers and were worthy examples to those who were entrusted to them. Every saint has been called to inherit God's glory. However, faithful ministers will be rewarded the crown of glory by God Himself. There are particular characteristics mentioned that indicate the reason why God will reward them with such a crown — willingness and example.

No Cross means No Crown

> *When they had twisted a crown of thorns, they put it on His head, and a reed in His right hand. And they bowed the knee before Him and mocked Him, saying, 'Hail, King of the Jews!'* — Matthew 27:29

Charles Spurgeon said, 'There are no crown-wearers in Heaven who were not cross-bearers here below.' Jesus' life demonstrated the truth for this principle, no cross means no crown. After humbling Himself by leaving Heaven, Jesus then further humbled

> **'There are no crown-wearers in Heaven who were not cross-bearers here below.'**

Himself to death on The Cross. What does The Cross symbolize? It is the humbling process you pass through in your obedience to God. It is the surrender of your will in obedience to God. In the garden of Gethsemane, Christ connects The Cross to God's will when He was praying. We must also pray and ask God to reveal His purpose to us, regardless of whether it may challenge us or be difficult. Though for the persecuted church they may bear a physical cross, every disciple of Jesus must carry their cross. This cross is a symbol of the suffering and ridicule, the persecution and self-denial that those who follow Jesus must bear. Christ no longer wears a crown of thorns but a crown of glory. Those who bear their cross on earth will be also crowned in Heaven.

CONCLUSION: DO NOT LET ANYONE STEAL YOUR CROWN!

> 'Behold, I am coming quickly! Hold fast what you have, that no one may take your crown." — Revelation 3:11

> 'For many deceivers have gone out into the world who do not confess Jesus Christ as coming in the flesh. This is a deceiver and an antichrist. Look to yourselves that we do not lose those things we worked for, but that we may receive a full reward.' — 2 John 1:7-8

Crowns can be lost or stolen. We are warned in the above scriptures 'hold fast' or 'look to ourselves that we do not lose the things we worked for'. This gives us the understanding that if we do not continue in faith and guard ourselves, we could lose our eternal reward. As Christians, we must not be ignorant of the plan of the enemy to make us lose our reward. We must have a militant approach and an eternal perspective. The bible says the enemy seeks to steal, kill and destroy. This kind of thief seeks to things that are much more valuable that money or gold, but joy, peace, faith and purity. Do not sit back but contend for you reward, guard your heart and as it says in 1 Timothy 6:12 'Fight the good fight of faith, lay hold on eternal life.' I pray that as you have become more aware of the eternal, holy fear will provoke you to live a life of purpose in Jesus. Do not procrastinate, live for Jesus today and make your days count!

CHAPTER 8 — ETERNAL JUDGMENT: PERSONAL STUDY

1. Scripture to remember is 2 Corinthians 5:9-11 and 1 Corinthians 3:11-15

2. List five benefits of an eternal perspective. In your own words explain why they are important.

   _____

   _____

   _____

3. According to the following scriptures, what will judgement be based on? Who will be our judge? John 12:47-48, John 5:22, Romans 2:16, Matthew 12:36

   _____

   _____

   _____

4. List the 5 Crowns mentioned in the last chapter. Describe them in your own words. Reflect on the rewards spoken of in Revelations 2-3

   _____

   _____

   _____

   _____

5. According to the following scriptures, Can we have boldness on the Day of Judgement? If yes, give practical application of how we can do so. 1 John 4:17, 2 Corinthians 5:9-11 and 1 Peter 1:17, and Matthew 18:21-35

   _____

   _____

   _____

   _____

END NOTE: GOING ON TO PERFECTION

'Therefore, leaving the discussion of the elementary principles of Christ, let us go on to perfection....' — Hebrews 6:1

INTRODUCTION

Is no one perfect? Well in the world's definition of perfect this may be the case. However, God's objective is for His children to be perfect. This would put immense pressure or even be intimidating if you do not understand what God's definition of perfection is. As we conclude, lets look at what the biblical meaning of perfection is, that you may go onto perfection in Jesus name.

WHAT IS GOD'S DEFINITION OF PERFECTION?

The word perfect in Greek is 'teleios' which means complete in growth, mental and moral character, to be of full age, a man perfect. It comes from a primary root word *'telos'* which means the conclusion of an act or state, the final result, purpose or finality. In other words, God's definition of perfection is about you being complete in the intended state for which you were created. Perfection in God's definition is about you being complete in your identity and because of this functioning in your purpose. The world's definition of perfection is about simply being immaculate, but God's definition is about identity, design, completeness and function.

> *'Gods definition of perfection is about you being complete in the intended state for which you were created.'*

'But I say to you, love your enemies, bless those who curse you, do good to those who hate you, and pray for those who spitefully use you and persecute you, that you may be sons of your Father in heaven; for He makes His sun rise on the evil and on the good, and sends rain on the just and on the unjust.

For if you love those who love you, what reward have you? Do not even the tax collectors do the same? And if you greet your brethren only, what do you do more than others? Do not even the tax collectors do so? Therefore you shall be perfect, just as your Father in heaven is perfect.' — Matthew 5:44-48

From the scripture above Jesus commands that if you love others and pray for those who use you, then you will be just as perfect as God. How? Because God has made us in His image and likeness (Genesis 1:26). To be made in the image of God means to be made in the image of Love. Because this is our identity, we have the ability to function in divine love towards other, even if they are hostile or treat us spitefully. By walking in our God given identity and functioning in this way, God declares we are perfect as He is. Simply by walking in your identity and functioning as God's child.

IDENTITY

From the natural human nature, we tend to base our identity and perception of worth from things like country of origin, ability, body shape, bank account, clothing design and job role.

Though these things have their place and purpose, they are temporary and basing your value and security on them leads to instability and destruction. The Gospel reveals that the foundation of our identity is God's unconditional love and righteousness He has gifted us through Jesus Christ (1 Peter 1:13). We are reborn into a supernatural nature/identity and are no longer merely men and women whose identity is primarily based on the things on Earth (Psalm 82:6).

This does not stop you from living on earth or having day-to-day needs and even having material things. However, Christ is now the source of your identity and no matter what, you can overcome life challenges through Him (Philippians 3:11-13). This also means that God is eternal and so we have an unchanging eternal foundation to base our identity, perceptions of security, value - even when things around us change. In fact, it is this that protects us from external things like job role, finance or when people's opinions say otherwise. This brings a distinction and provides a doorway to share the Gospel with others.

CONCLUSION

The principles, testimonies and insights contained in this book are to empower you to advance onto Gods perfection. For some readers, it may be inspiring by reminding you of things God has already taught you. For other readers, it may be provoking and challenge you to study further. For others, it may be a call to give your life to Jesus. Whatever the case I would encourage you to trust in Jesus and build your life on obedience to His word. The foundation is just the beginning; God's end result for you is perfection in Him. I pray that God perfects the work He started in you in Jesus' name. God bless you.

Emmanuel Adeseko

BIBLIOGRAPHY

CHAPTER 2
Hession, R. (2003). The Power of God's Grace. Wendover: Rickfords Hill Publishing, Buckinghamshire.

CHAPTER 3
AZ Quotes. (2016, April 15). *John G. Lake*. Retrieved 2016 from AZ Quotes: http://www.azquotes.com/quote/890176

CHAPTER 7
Spurgen, C. (2013). The Complete Works of Charles Spurgeon: Volume 48, Sermons 2760-2811 London: DelmarvaPublications

ABOUT THE AUTHOR

Emmanuel Adeseko is passionate to see people reconciled to God a grow in an intimate relationship with Jesus. He is an author, speak pastor and believes that identity in Christ inspires authority to reign in li He is the founder of New Covenant Ministries based in Birmingham UK. also has the opportunity to speak in various conferences across the U seeing lives transformed by the Gospel.

For more info, invites or bookings: newcovenant@live.co.uk

Facebook: Emmanuel Adeseko

Website: Newcovenantministries.co.uk

Made in the USA
Charleston, SC
14 October 2016